TABLE

INTRODUCTION: WELCOMING INVITATION

C ome with us on this mysterious excursion through the book that enables you to relive those epic years that framed the whole world and whose effects remain on the minds and hearts of us even today. Whether you fondly remember rock and roll, the golden age of television, the movie stars legend, or the sports legends who will never be forgotten, you will find yourself immersed in an environment that rekindles the former awe and views in the 1950s and 1990s.

Here comes the twist! It's time to bridge your connections with the past by returning to when the noise, styles, and events brought unity. The duration of funny 600 trivia questions will put memories to the test, and if you have a friend by your side who scores more than you on the quiz, there are high chances you will end up learning something new about the decades you thought you were familiar with.

With every chapter, you will enter a wheel of time, whether past, present, or future. You'd be free to write down your experiences and thoughts from that decade and the trends. Writers are indulged in making notes on the blank leaves at the end of the chapter or on those of separate papers to maintain the book as it is for future applications. Even though the different subjects are images, titles, and episodes from music, television, sports, fashion, and important international events, you will have many memories coming out, pushing you to discuss things and be happy.

Thus, kindly come along with your close ones, put your hearts on unveiling the mysteries, and relish the adventure into the past. Why not take turns entertaining each other with our intellectual jousts, post some of our stories on our website, and relive the experiences that always make us feel much younger? Enjoy!

The pages of this trivia book trigger a nostalgic journey that spans every decade and serves as a blueprint for the cultural experience we now enjoy, be it riveting songs from music festivals to the golden TV era. It leads us through travel starting in the 90s decade, reflecting on the past, and reminding the emotions and the community that are unforgettable. For every question featured, readers conclude that they can be the hero of their own story, thus multiplying the number of their new friends and providing deeper insights into their lives. The book is presented in a timeline mode, chronologically showcasing a kaleidoscope of iconic events, followed by quizzical questions that will put to the test the reader while at the same time providing moments of relaxation. With each one of the chapters end, readers will have an opportunity to review their journey personally on the pages devoted especially to one's thoughts and memories.

FIT FOREVER

The 1950s: A Dawn of Cultural Revolution

T he 1950s became a decade of sublime boom, and the world experienced quite a transformation. The post-World War II feeling of optimism pushed the economies forward, and during the 1950s, the US was dominated, mainly due to the housing boom and consumerism. In this decade, rock and roll music was born, and it has been identified with such heroes and heroines as Elvis Presley and Chuck Berry, who have advanced the cultural revolution of the youth. Television was indigenized by households and hosted all sorts of shows that contributed tremendously to the formation of public opinions and entertained the masses. Although the decade was characterized by the suburban utopia, on the underlying side, it was also a time of deep political division arising from the Cold War and the beginning of the Civil Rights Movement and, therefore, the stage setting for the social changes yet to come.

1950s Trivia Questions

1. WHAT YEAR DID THE FIRST EPISODE OF "I LOVE LUCY" AIR?

    a) 1949
    b) 1951
    c) 1952
    d) 1950

2. WHO WAS THE LEAD ACTOR IN THE MOVIE "REBEL WITHOUT A CAUSE"?

    a) Marlon Brando
    b) Paul Newman
    c) Elvis Presley
    d) James Dean

3. WHICH ROCK AND ROLL ICON IS KNOWN FOR HITS LIKE "HEARTBREAK HOTEL" AND "HOUND DOG"?

a) Frank Sinatra
b) Buddy Holly
c) Michael Jackson
d) Elvis Presley

4. WHAT MAJOR EVENT MARKED THE BEGINNING OF THE CIVIL RIGHTS MOVEMENT IN 1955?

a) The signing of the Civil Rights Act
b) Martin Luther King Jr.'s "I Have a Dream" speech
c) The integration of Central High School in Little Rock
d) The Montgomery Bus Boycott

5. WHAT GROUNDBREAKING MEDICAL INVENTION DID DR. JONAS SALK DEVELOP IN 1955?

a) The X-ray machines
b) Penicillin
c) The MRI machines
d) The polio vaccine

6. WHO WAS THE SOVIET PREMIER DURING THE LAUNCH OF SPUTNIK?

a) Vladimir Lenin
b) Joseph Stalin
c) Mikhail Gorbachev
d) Nikita Khrushchev\

7. WHICH U.S. PRESIDENT LAUNCHED THE INTERSTATE HIGHWAY SYSTEM IN THE 1950S?

a) Harry S. Truman
b) John F. Kennedy
c) Lyndon B. Johnson
d) Dwight D. Eisenhower

8. WHO WROTE THE PLAY "A STREETCAR NAMED DESIRE"?

   a) Arthur Miller
   b) Eugene O'Neill
   c) Edward Albee
   d) Tennessee Williams

9. WHAT WAS THE FIRST LAUNCHED INTO ORBIT BY THE SOVIET UNION IN 1957?

   a) Explorer
   b) Voyager
   c) Hubble
   d) Sputnik

10. WHAT COMPANY INTRODUCED THE FIRST CREDIT CARD IN 1950?

   a) American Express
   b) Visa
   c) MasterCard
   d) Diners Club

11. WHICH GAME SHOW PREMIERED IN 1956, ASKING CONTESTANTS TO GUESS HIDDEN WORDS THROUGH CLEVER QUESTIONING?

   a) The Price Is Right
   b) Password
   c) What's My Line?
   d) To Tell the Truth

12. WHAT U.S. SUPREME COURT CASE DECLARED SCHOOL SEGREGATION UNCONSTITUTIONAL IN 1954?

   a) Plessy v. Ferguson
   b) Marbury v. Madison
   c) Brown v. Board of Education
   d) Roe v. Wade

13. WHICH MOVIE CELEBRITY SANG "DIAMONDS ARE A GIRL'S BEST FRIEND" IN GENTLEMEN PREFER BLONDES?

    a) Audrey Hepburn
    b) Marilyn Monroe
    c) Elizabeth Taylor
    d) Grace Kelly

14. WHO WAS KNOWN AS THE "KING OF ROCK AND ROLL" AND DEBUTED ON NATIONAL T.V. ON THE ED SULLIVAN SHOW?

    a) Chuck Berry
    b) Johnny Cash
    c) Jerry Lee Lewis
    d) Elvis Presley

15. WHICH MUSICAL FEATURING THE SONG "I COULD HAVE DANCED ALL NIGHT" PREMIERED IN 1956?

    a) The Sound of Music
    b) West Side Story
    c) My Fair Lady
    d) Carousel

16. WHAT POLITICAL EVENT MARKED THE DIVISION BETWEEN NORTH AND SOUTH KOREA IN THE 1950S?

    a) The signing of the Korean Armistice Agreement
    b) The end of World War II
    c) The Korean War's beginning
    d) The Vietnam War's beginning

17. WHAT DANCE CRAZE, MADE POPULAR BY CHUBBY CHECKER, HAD PEOPLE TWISTING THE NIGHT AWAY?

    a) The Mashed Potato
    b) The Moonwalk
    c) The Twist
    d) The Cha-Cha Slide

18. WHICH COUNTRY BECAME THE FIRST TO GIVE WOMEN THE RIGHT TO VOTE?

a) United States
b) United Kingdom
c) New Zealand
d) Australia

19. WHAT AFRICAN-AMERICAN PERFORMER BECAME FAMOUS FOR HER PERFORMANCE IN PORGY AND BESS?

a) Diana Ross
b) Ella Fitzgerald
c) Leontyne Price
d) Billie Holiday

20. WHICH CAR MANUFACTURER INTRODUCED THE CORVETTE, AMERICA'S SPORTS CAR, IN 1953?

a) Ford
b) Chrysler
c) Chevrolet
d) Cadillac

21. WHO BECAME THE FIRST FEMALE PILOT TO GO THROUGH THE SOUND BARRIER IN 1953?

a) Amelia Earhart
b) Harriet Quimby
c) Jacqueline Cochran
d) Bessie Coleman

22. WHAT WELL-KNOWN SITCOM FEATURED TWO NEIGHBORS NAMED FRED AND ETHEL MERTZ?

a) the honeymooners
b) I Love Lucy
c) Bewitched
d) The Andy Griffith Show

23. WHICH T.V. SHOW FIRST INTRODUCED A SUPERHERO TO A YOUNG AUDIENCE IN THE 1950S?

a) Batman
b) The Lone Ranger
c) Superman
d) Captain America

24. WHO WAS KNOWN FOR THE POPULAR SINGLE "BLUEBERRY HILL" AND OTHER HITS IN THE 1950S?

a) Chuck Berry
b) Fats Domino
c) Little Richard
d) Elvis Presley

25. WHAT PIECE OF LEGISLATION, PASSED IN 1957, AIMED TO INCREASE VOTER REGISTRATION AMONG AFRICAN AMERICANS?

a) Civil Rights Act of 1957
b) Voting Rights Act of 1965
c) Civil Rights Act of 1964
d) Equal Rights Amendment

26. WHAT MUSIC GENRE ORIGINATED IN THE DEEP SOUTH AND BECAME POPULAR NATIONWIDE IN THE 1950S?

a) Blues
b) Jazz
c) Rock and Roll
d) Gospel

27. WHICH WORLD LEADER OVERSAW THE HUNGARIAN REVOLUTION OF 1956?

a) Nikita Khrushchev
b) Dwight D. Eisenhower
c) Joseph Stalin
d) John F. Kennedy

28. WHICH ICONIC BRITISH ACTRESS STARRED IN ROMAN HOLIDAY IN 1953?

a) Elizabeth Taylor
b) Vivien Leigh
c) Audrey Hepburn
d) Julie Andrews

29. WHAT HOLIDAY CHARACTER MADE HIS FIRST APPEARANCE IN THE MACY'S THANKSGIVING DAY PARADE IN 1957?

a) Santa Claus
b) Rudolph the Red-Nosed Reindeer
c) Frosty the Snowman
d) Charlie Brown

30. WHICH WELL-KNOWN T.V. HOST INTRODUCED ELVIS PRESLEY TO THE NATIONAL AUDIENCE IN THE MID-1950S?

a) Ed Sullivan
b) Johnny Carson
c) Dick Clark
d) Steve Allen

31. WHAT CONSUMER PRODUCT, FIRST INTRODUCED BY PROCTER & GAMBLE, REVOLUTIONIZED HOW PEOPLE CLEANED THEIR HOMES?

a) Swiffer
b) Mr. Clean
c) Tide
d) Lysol

32. WHAT POPULAR CEREAL BRAND USED A CARTOON ROOSTER AS ITS MASCOT IN THE 1950S?

a) Frosted Flakes
b) Froot Loops
c) Corn Flakes
d) Wheaties

33. WHAT LITERARY MAGAZINE DEBUTED IN 1953 AND BECAME A CORNERSTONE OF ADULT ENTERTAINMENT?

a) Playboy
b) Penthouse
c) Vanity Fair
d) Esquire

34. WHAT ICONIC FILM STARRING CHARLTON HESTON BECAME FAMOUS FOR ITS CHARIOT RACE IN 1959?

a) Spartacus
b) Ben-Hur
c) Cleopatra
d) The Ten Commandments

35. WHICH STYLE OF ARCHITECTURE, OFTEN ASSOCIATED WITH POSTWAR SUBURBAN HOMES, BECAME POPULAR IN THE 1950S?

a) Victorian
b) Ranch-style
c) Art Deco
d) Craftsman

36. WHO WERE THE FIRST AFRICAN-AMERICAN STUDENTS TO JOIN CENTRAL HIGH SCHOOL IN LITTLE ROCK, ARKANSAS, IN 1957?

a) The Freedom Riders
b) The Little Rock Nine
c) The Birmingham Six
d) The Greensboro Four

37. WHICH SOVIET LEADER REPLACED JOSEPH STALIN AFTER HE DIED IN 1953?

a) Leonid Brezhnev
b) Nikita Khrushchev
c) Mikhail Gorbachev
d) Vladimir Lenin

38. WHICH AFRICAN-AMERICAN BASEBALL PLAYER BROKE THE COLOR BARRIER WHEN HE JOINED THE MLB IN THE 1950S?

a) Hank Aaron
b) Willie Mays
c) Jackie Robinson
d) Satchel Paige

39. WHICH 1955 JAMES DEAN MOVIE FAMOUSLY PORTRAYED TEENAGE ANGST AND REBELLION?

a) Giant
b) East of Eden
c) Rebel Without a Cause
d) The Wild One

40. WHAT WAS THE FIRST COLOR TELEVISION NETWORK TO BEGIN BROADCASTING IN 1954?

a) NBC
b) CBS
c) ABC
d) Fox

41. WHAT POPULAR NOVEL BY J.D. SALINGER WAS PUBLISHED IN THE 1950S AND BECAME A CLASSIC?

a) To Kill a Mockingbird
b) The Catcher in the Rye
c) Lord of the Flies
d) On the Road

42. WHAT WAS THE FIRST FAST-FOOD CHAIN TO INTRODUCE A DRIVE-THRU SERVICE IN THE 1950S?

a) McDonald's
b) Burger King
c) In-N-Out Burger
d) Wendy's

43. WHICH AMERICAN AUTHOR WROTE ON THE ROAD, THE DEFINING WORK OF THE BEAT GENERATION?

a) Jack Kerouac
b) Allen Ginsberg
c) William S. Burroughs
d) Hunter S. Thompson

44. WHICH 1958 HORROR FILM BECAME A CULT CLASSIC AND FEATURED A MONSTROUS BLOB TERRORIZING A SMALL TOWN?

a) The Thing
b) The Blob
c) Invasion of the Body Snatchers
d) The Fly

45. WHAT SPORTS LEAGUE SAW THE BEGINNING OF ITS FIRST DYNASTY IN THE 1950S, LED BY THE BOSTON CELTICS?

a) NFL
b) NBA
c) MLB
d) NHL

46. WHICH T.V. SHOW WAS KNOWN FOR FEATURING A TALKING HORSE AND HIS HUMOROUS ADVENTURES?

a) Mister Ed
b) BoJack Horseman
c) My Little Pony
d) The Lone Ranger

47. WHAT WAS THE NAME OF THE NASA SPACE MISSION THAT AIMED TO PUT A MAN ON THE MOON IN THE 1950S?

a) Apollo Program
b) Gemini Program
c) Mercury Program
d) Artemis Program

48. WHICH AMERICAN SINGER WAS KNOWN FOR HIS SIGNATURE "HOWDY DOODY" GREETING?

a) Buffalo Bob Smith
b) Pat Boone
c) Buddy Holly
d) Gene Autry

49. WHAT BEST-SELLING NOVEL BY GRACE METALIOUS SHOCKED READERS WITH ITS PORTRAYAL OF SMALL-TOWN SECRETS IN THE 1950S?

a) Peyton Place
b) To Kill a Mockingbird
c) Atlas Shrugged
d) Lord of the Flies

50. WHICH U.S. PRESIDENT AUTHORIZED THE ESTABLISHMENT OF NASA IN 1958?

a) John F. Kennedy
b) Dwight D. Eisenhower
c) Lyndon B. Johnson
d) Richard Nixo

51. WHAT ICONIC JAZZ ALBUM BY MILES DAVIS BECAME A LANDMARK IN COOL JAZZ DURING THE 1950S?

a) Giant Steps
b) Blue Train
c) Kind of Blue
d) A Love Supreme

52. WHO WAS THE FIRST AFRICAN-AMERICAN WOMAN TO WIN THE OSCAR FOR BEST SUPPORTING ACTRESS IN 1950?

a) Dorothy Dandridge
b) Hattie McDaniel
c) Ethel Waters
d) Ruby Dee

53. WHICH SOCIAL MOVEMENT AIMED AT DEFENDING ARTISTS AND INTELLECTUALS AGAINST CENSORSHIP GREW IN THE 1950S?

a) The Free Speech Movement
b) The Civil Rights Movement
c) The Beat Movement
d) The Counterculture Movement

54. WHAT POPULAR DANCE CRAZE, NAMED AFTER A BALLROOM DANCE AND SWEEPING THE NATION, WAS PROMINENT IN THE 1950S?

a) The Tango
b) The Waltz
c) The Mambo
d) The Foxtrot

55. WHICH NEW MODE OF TRANSPORTATION FIRST TOOK OFF IN THE 1950S AND SHORTENED TRAVEL TIME BETWEEN CITIES?

a) High-speed trains
b) Commercial jet airplanes
c) Electric cars
d) Hovercraft

56. WHAT EVENT BROUGHT THOUSANDS OF SOLDIERS AND THEIR FAMILIES HOME IN THE EARLY 1950S?

a) The end of the Korean War
b) The end of World War II
c) The end of the Vietnam War
d) The end of the Cold War

57. WHAT POPULAR PLAY BY ARTHUR MILLER CRITICIZED THE ANTI-COMMUNIST HYSTERIA OF THE 1950S?

a) Death of a Salesman
b) The Crucible
c) A View from the Bridge
d) All My Sons

58. WHICH BROADWAY MUSICAL FAMOUSLY FEATURED A GANG BATTLE BETWEEN THE JETS AND THE SHARKS?

a) Grease
b) West Side Story
c) Rent
d) Chicago

59. WHAT INFLUENTIAL SCIENTIFIC DISCOVERY CHANGED MEDICINE AND TREATMENT PROTOCOLS IN THE 1950S?

a) The discovery of penicillin
b) The development of the polio vaccine
c) The invention of the MRI machine
d) The creation of insulin

60. WHICH LEADER, "IL DUCE," SIGNIFICANTLY IMPACTED ITALIAN POLITICS IN THE 1950S?

a) Benito Mussolini
b) Alcide De Gasperi
c) Giuseppe Saragat
d) Enrico Berlinguer

61. WHICH ATHLETE FAMOUSLY WON GOLD MEDALS IN THE OLYMPIC DECATHLON IN THE 1950S?

a) Jesse Owens
b) Carl Lewis
c) Bob Mathias
d) Jim Thor

62. WHAT AMERICAN ROAD BECAME FAMOUS FOR CONNECTING TRAVELERS COMING FROM CHICAGO TO LOS ANGELES IN THE 1950S?

a) Pacific Coast Highway
b) Route 66
c) Interstate 70
d) The Lincoln Highway

63. WHICH FAST-FOOD CHAIN INTRODUCED THE FILET-O-FISH SANDWICH IN THE 1950S?

a) Wendy's
b) McDonald's
c) Burger King
d) KFC

64. WHICH BRITISH CAR MANUFACTURER LAUNCHED THE WORLD'S FIRST MASS-PRODUCED SPORTS CAR IN 1953?

a) Jaguar
b) Aston Martin
c) Bentley
d) MG

65. WHAT ADVERTISING TECHNIQUE, FIRST USED ON TELEVISION IN THE 1950S, BECAME POPULAR FOR SELLING PRODUCTS?

a) Celebrity endorsements
b) Infomercials
c) Product placement
d) Direct response TV

66. WHICH FAMED TALK SHOW HOST EARNED THE NICKNAME "KING OF LATE NIGHT" IN THE 1950S?

a) Johnny Carson
b) Ed Sullivan
c) Jack Paar
d) Steve Allen

67. WHAT WAS THE FIRST NATIONWIDE TELEVISION BROADCAST IN THE 1950S, REACHING MILLIONS OF AMERICANS?

a) The presidential inauguration
b) The first Super Bowl
c) The Queen's Coronation
d) A World Series game

68. WHICH 1950S COMEDIAN WAS KNOWN FOR HIS DEADPAN HUMOR AND SIGNATURE "WELL, I'LL BE DARNED" CATCHPHRASE?

a) Bob Hope
b) Jack Benny
c) Rodney Dangerfield
d) George Burns

69. WHICH AMERICAN ARTIST PAINTED THE ICONIC CAMPBELL'S SOUP CANS SERIES, POPULARIZING POP ART IN THE 1950S?

a) Andy Warhol
b) Roy Lichtenstein
c) Jasper Johns
d) Robert Rauschenberg

70. WHAT POPULAR METHOD FOR RECORDING SOUND BECAME WIDELY ADOPTED IN THE 1950S?

a) 8-track tapes
b) Vinyl records
c) Magnetic tape
d) Phonograph cylinders

71. WHICH U.S. STATE BECAME THE LAST TO JOIN THE UNION IN THE 1950S?

a) Alaska
b) Hawaii
c) Arizona
d) New Mexico

72. WHAT 1956 ALFRED HITCHCOCK FILM STARRED JAMES STEWART IN A STORY ABOUT VOYEURISM AND OBSESSION?

a) Psycho
b) Rear Window
c) Vertigo
d) The Man Who Knew Too Much

73. WHAT FAMOUS BLACK-AND-WHITE FILM INTRODUCED GODZILLA TO THE WORLD IN 1954?

a) King Kong
b) Godzilla
c) The Beast from 20,000 Fathoms
d) Them!

74. WHICH SOUTHERN U.S. STATE SAW A SIGNIFICANT POPULATION BOOM IN THE 1950S DUE TO INDUSTRIAL GROWTH AND SUBURBANIZATION?

a) Georgia
b) Texas
c) Florida
d) Alabama

75. WHICH BASEBALL PLAYER SET A RECORD FOR CONSECUTIVE GAMES WITH A HIT THAT STOOD FOR OVER 50 YEARS?

a) Babe Ruth
b) Joe DiMaggio
c) Mickey Mantle
d) Ted William

76. WHAT MAJOR DEPARTMENT STORE, STILL PROMINENT TODAY, REVOLUTIONIZED RETAIL IN THE 1950S?

a) Macy's
b) Sears
c) J.C. Penney
d) Nordstrom

77. WHICH HORROR FILM FEATURED VINCENT PRICE AS A MAD WAX SCULPTOR IN 1953?

a) House of Wax
b) The Fly
c) House on Haunted Hill
d) The Tingler

78. WHAT MAJOR MUSIC FESTIVAL IN HARLEM, NEW YORK, BROUGHT JAZZ TO A WIDER AUDIENCE IN THE 1950S?

a) The Harlem Renaissance Festival
b) The Newport Jazz Festival
c) The Harlem Jazz Festival
d) The Cotton Club Festival

79. WHICH EUROPEAN COUNTRY EXPERIENCED A MASSIVE BABY BOOM DUE TO POSTWAR ECONOMIC GROWTH IN THE 1950S?

a) Germany
b) United Kingdom
c) France
d) Italy

80. WHAT ANIMATED DISNEY CLASSIC ABOUT A YOUNG DEER FIRST ENCHANTED AUDIENCES IN THE 1950S?

a) Bambi
b) Snow White and the Seven Dwarfs
c) Cinderella
d) Peter Pan

81. WHAT FAMOUS AMUSEMENT PARK OPENED ITS DOORS IN CALIFORNIA IN 1955?

a) Six Flags
b) Disneyland
c) Knott's Berry Farm
d) Universal Studios

82. WHICH AMERICAN FOOTBALL LEAGUE EXPANDED ITS REACH WITH NEW TEAMS IN THE 1950S?

a) The American Football League
b) The National Football League
c) The United Football League
d) The Canadian Football League

83. WHAT POPULAR FASHION ACCESSORY BECAME SYNONYMOUS WITH HIGH-END ELEGANCE AND CHIC STYLE IN THE 1950S?

a) Fedora hats
b) Leather gloves
c) Pearl necklaces
d) Silk scarves

84. WHICH POLITICAL MOVEMENT LED BY SENATOR JOSEPH MCCARTHY INVESTIGATED SUSPECTED COMMUNISTS IN THE 1950S?

a) The Red Scare
b) The McCarthy Hearings
c) The Cold War Investigations
d) The Anti-Communist League

85. WHAT STYLE OF JAZZ, KNOWN FOR ITS COOL AND RELAXED SOUND, EMERGED AS A SIGNIFICANT TREND IN THE 1950S?

a) Bebop
b) Swing
c) Cool jazz
d) Hard bop

86. WHICH CARTOON SERIES INTRODUCED A FAMOUS CAT-AND-MOUSE DUO WHO ENGAGED IN COMEDIC PURSUITS?

a) Looney Tunes
b) Tom and Jerry
c) Mickey and Minnie
d) Sylvester and Tweety

87. WHICH U.S. STATE SAW THE GREATEST EXPANSION OF ITS HIGHWAY SYSTEM DUE TO RAPID URBANIZATION IN THE 1950S?

a) California
b) New York
c) Texas
d) Florida

88. WHAT HOLIDAY MOVIE BECAME A CLASSIC DURING THE 1950S
AND STILL DELIGHTS FAMILIES TODAY?

a) Miracle on 34th Street
b) White Christmas
c) It's a Wonderful Life
d) A Christmas Caro

89. WHICH NATIONAL MONUMENT WAS EXPANDED TO INCLUDE TWO
ADDITIONAL PRESIDENTS IN THE 1950S?

a) The Lincoln Memorial
b) The Washington Monument
c) Mount Rushmore
d) The Jefferson Memorial

90. WHICH LITERARY GENRE POPULARIZED BY AUTHORS LIKE
MICKEY SPILLANE BECAME WIDELY READ IN THE 1950S?

a) Science fiction
b) Mystery
c) Romance
d) Hard-boiled detective

91. WHAT FAMOUS NOVELIST PUBLISHED EAST OF EDEN IN THE 1950S,
EXAMINING FAMILY DYNAMICS?

a) Ernest Hemingway
b) John Steinbeck
c) F. Scott Fitzgerald
d) William Faulkner

92. WHICH FILM ACTRESS WAS KNOWN FOR HER DRAMATIC ROLES IN
SUDDEN FEAR AND WHATEVER HAPPENED TO BABY JANE?

a) Audrey Hepburn
b) Bette Davis
c) Katharine Hepburn
d) Marilyn Monroe

93. WHAT WAS THE NAME OF THE U.S. AIRCRAFT THAT DROPPED THE FIRST HYDROGEN BOMB IN THE 1950S?

a) Enola Gay
b) B-52 Stratofortress
c) B-29 Superfortress
d) B-36 Peacemaker

94. WHICH U.S. CITY SAW THE RISE OF HIGH-RISE RESIDENTIAL BUILDINGS DUE TO THE HOUSING SHORTAGE IN THE 1950S?

a) Los Angeles
b) New York City
c) Chicago
d) San Francisco

95. WHAT EUROPEAN COUNTRY HOSTED THE FIRST EUROVISION SONG CONTEST IN 1956?

a) United Kingdom
b) Switzerland
c) France
d) Italy

96. WHAT POPULAR T.V. GAME SHOW AWARDED LARGE CASH PRIZES TO CONTESTANTS ANSWERING TRIVIA QUESTIONS IN THE 1950S?

a) The Price Is Right
b) Jeopardy!
c) The $64,000 Question
d) Who Wants to Be a Millionaire

97. WHICH BASEBALL TEAM WON THE WORLD SERIES FIVE TIMES DURING THE 1950S?

a) New York Yankees
b) Boston Red Sox
c) Los Angeles Dodgers
d) Chicago Cubs

98. WHAT WAS THE NAME OF THE FIRST U.S. SATELLITE LAUNCHED IN 1958 TO ORBIT THE EARTH?

a) Explorer 1
b) Vanguard 1
c) Sputnik 1
d) Telstar

99. WHAT ASIAN COUNTRY'S ARMISTICE AGREEMENT HELPED BRING PEACE AFTER YEARS OF CONFLICT IN THE 1950S?

a) Vietnam
b) Korea
c) China
d) Japan

100. WHICH COLD WAR ORGANIZATION WAS FORMED IN 1955 TO COUNTER THE GROWING INFLUENCE OF NATO?

a) The Warsaw Pact
b) The United Nations
c) The League of Nations
d) The Shanghai Cooperation

101. WHAT CONSUMER PRODUCT HELPED SPARK A HEALTH REVOLUTION DUE TO CONCERNS ABOUT HYGIENE AND CLEANLINESS?

a) Vacuum cleaner
b) Disposable diapers
c) Antibacterial soap
d) Toothpaste

102. WHICH MAJOR U.S. CITY SAW THE CREATION OF ONE OF THE WORLD'S TALLEST SKYSCRAPERS IN THE 1950S?

a) Chicago
b) New York City
c) Los Angeles
d) Houston

103. WHAT FAMOUS POLITICAL LEADER GAVE HIS FAREWELL SPEECH URGING AMERICANS TO BEWARE OF THE MILITARY-INDUSTRIAL COMPLEX?

a) John F. Kennedy
b) Lyndon B. Johnson
c) Dwight D. Eisenhower
d) Harry S. Truman

104. WHICH NEWSPAPER PUBLISHER BECAME KNOWN FOR HIS CONTROVERSIAL COVERAGE OF POLITICAL SCANDALS AND CELEBRITY GOSSIP?

a) Joseph Pulitzer
b) William Randolph Hearst
c) Rupert Murdoch
d) Robert McCormick

105. WHAT CONSUMER MAGAZINE, KNOWN FOR ITS DISTINCTIVE COVER, BECAME AN ICON OF AMERICAN CULTURE IN THE 1950S?

a) Time
b) Life
c) Playboy
d) Reader's Digest

106. WHAT NOTABLE SCIENTIFIC BREAKTHROUGHS CHANGED THE WAY WE UNDERSTOOD GENETICS IN THE 1950S?

a) Discovery of DNA's double helix structure
b) Development of the polio vaccine
c) Invention of the MRI machine
d) Launch of the first artificial satellite

107. WHICH COLD WAR POLICY, ARTICULATED BY PRESIDENT TRUMAN, SOUGHT TO STEM THE SPREAD OF COMMUNISM IN THE 1950S?

a) The Marshall Plan
b) The Truman Doctrine
c) The Eisenhower Doctrine
d) The Monroe Doctrine

108. WHICH WELL-KNOWN SCIENTIST HELPED POPULARIZE QUANTUM MECHANICS AND RELATIVITY THROUGH HIS WORK IN THE 1950S?

a) Niels Bohr
b) Albert Einstein
c) Richard Feynman
d) Werner Heisenber

109. WHAT ICONIC FASHION DESIGNER INTRODUCED THE "NEW LOOK," INFLUENCING WOMEN'S CLOTHING THROUGHOUT THE DECADE?

a) Coco Chanel
b) Christian Dior
c) Yves Saint Laurent
d) Giorgio Arman

110. WHICH ASIAN NATION, DEVASTATED BY WAR, LAUNCHED ITS FIRST ECONOMIC RECOVERY PLAN IN THE 1950S?

a) China
b) Japan
c) Vietnam
d) Korea

111. WHAT WORLD-FAMOUS POP ART PAINTING BY ROY LICHTENSTEIN POPULARIZED COMIC BOOK IMAGERY IN THE 1950S?

a) Whaam!
b) Drowning Girl
c) Look Mickey
d) Campbell's Soup Cans

112. WHICH PIONEERING CIVIL RIGHTS LEADER URGED NONVIOLENT RESISTANCE TO SEGREGATION IN THE 1950S?

a) Malcolm X
b) Martin Luther King Jr.
c) Rosa Parks
d) Fred Shuttlesworth

113. WHAT LONG-RUNNING TV DRAMA INTRODUCED VIEWERS TO COURTROOM LAW AND DETECTIVE WORK IN THE 1950S?

a) The Twilight Zone
b) Perry Mason
c) Dragnet
d) Alfred Hitchcock Presents

114. WHICH SHORT-LIVED POLITICAL MOVEMENT SOUGHT TO MAINTAIN SEGREGATION BY ADVOCATING "MASSIVE RESISTANCE" IN THE 1950S?

a) The Civil Rights Movement
b) The Dixiecrat Movement
c) The Southern Manifesto
d) The Ku Klux Klan

115. WHAT NEW MUSIC GENRE EVOLVED FROM A COMBINATION OF JAZZ, GOSPEL, AND RHYTHM AND BLUES IN THE 1950S?

a) Rock and Roll
b) Hip Hop
c) Disco
d) Soul

116. WHAT POPULAR VARIETY SHOW ENTERTAINED VIEWERS WITH COMEDY SKITS, CELEBRITY GUESTS, AND MUSICAL NUMBERS IN THE 1950S?

a) Saturday Night Live
b) The Ed Sullivan Show
c) The Carol Burnett Show
d) The Tonight Show

117. WHAT LEGENDARY BASEBALL PLAYER EARNED THE NICKNAME "HAMMERIN' HANK" DUE TO HIS POWERFUL HITTING IN THE 1950S?

a) Mickey Mantle
b) Babe Ruth
c) Hank Aaron
d) Willie Mays

118. WHICH TV NEWS ANCHOR BECAME THE AUTHORITATIVE VOICE OF AMERICA, DELIVERING MAJOR HEADLINES IN THE 1950S?

a) Walter Cronkite
b) Edward R. Murrow
c) Dan Rather
d) Tom Brokaw

119. WHAT INFLUENTIAL NOVEL BY RALPH ELLISON EXPLORED RACE, IDENTITY, AND SOCIETY IN POST-WAR AMERICA?

a) Invisible Man
b) Native Son
c) Go Tell It on the Mountain
d) Another Country

120. WHICH U.S. STATE SAW ITS FIRST PROFESSIONAL BASKETBALL TEAM REACH THE PLAYOFFS IN THE LATE 1950S?

a) New York
b) California
c) Illinois
d) Massachusetts

Answer for 1950s

1. b) 1951

2. d) James Dean

3. d) Elvis Presley

4. d) The Montgomery Bus Boycott

5. d) The polio vaccine

6. d) Nikita Khrushchev

7. d) Dwight D. Eisenhower

8. d) Tennessee Williams

9. d) Sputnik 1

10. d) Diners Club

11. b) Password

12. c) Brown v. Board of Education

13. b) Marilyn Monroe

14. d) Elvis Presley

15. c) My Fair Lady

16. b) The end of World War II

17. c) The Twist

18. c) New Zealand

19. c) Leontyne Price

20. c) Chevrolet

21. c) Jacqueline Cochran

22. b) I Love Lucy

23. c) Superman

24. b) Fats Domino

25. a) The Civil Rights Act of 1957

26. c) Rock and Roll

27. a) Nikita Khrushchev

28. c) Audrey Hepburn

29. b) Rudolph the Red-Nosed Reindeer

30. a) Ed Sullivan

31. b) Tide

32. c) Corn Flakes

33. a) Playboy

34. b) Ben-Hur

35. b) Ranch-style

36. b) The Little Rock Nine

37. b) Nikita Khrushchev

38. c) Jackie Robinson

39. c) Rebel Without a Cause

40. a) NBC

41. b) The Catcher in the Rye

42. c) In-N-Out Burger

43. a) Jack Kerouac

44. b) The Blob

45. b) NBA

46. a) Mister Ed

47. a) Apollo Program

48. a) Buffalo Bob Smith

49. a) Peyton Place

50. b) Dwight D. Eisenhower

51. c) Kind of Blue

52. b) Hattie McDaniel

53. c) The Beat Movement

54. c) The Mambo

55. b) Commercial Jet airplanes

56. a) The end of the Korean War

57. b) The Crucible

58. b) West Side Story

59. b) The development of the polio vaccine

60. a) Benito Mussolini

61. c) Bob Mathias

62. b) Route 66

63. b) McDonald's

64. d) MG

65. a) Celebrity endorsements

66. c) Jack Paar

67. a) The presidential inauguration

68. b) Jack Benny

69. a) Andy Warhol

70. c) Magnetic Tape

71. b) Hawaii

72. b) Rear Window

73. b) Godzilla

74. c) Florida

75. b) Joe DiMaggio

76. b) Sears

77. a) House of Wax

78. b) The Newport Jazz Festival

79. c) France

80. a) Bambi

81. b) Disneyland

82. b) NFL

83. c) Pearls Pearl necklaces

84. b) The McCarthy Hearings

85. c) Cool Jazz

86. b) Tom and Jerry

87. a) California

88. b) White Christmas

89. c) Mount Rushmore

90. d) Hard-boiled detective

91. b) John Steinbeck

92. b) Bette Davis

93. d) B-36 Peacemaker

94. b) New York City

95. b) Switzerland

96. c) The $64,000 Question

97. a) New York Yankees

98. a) Explorer 1

99. c) Korea

100. b) Warsaw Pact

101. c) Antibacterial Soap

102. b) New York City

103. c) Dwight D. Eisenhower

104. b) William Randolph Hearst

105. b) Life

106. a) Discovery of DNA's double helix structure

107. b) The Truman Doctrine

108. b) Albert Einstein

109. b) Christian Dior

110. c) Japan

111. b) Look Mickey

112. b) Martin Luther King Jr.

113. b) Perry Mason

114. c) The Southern Manifesto

115. b) Rock and Roll

116. b) The Ed Sullivan Show

117. a) Hank Aaron

118. a) Walter Cronkite

119. a) Invisible Man

120. b) California

CHAPTER 2

ENTERTAINMENT AND MEDIA

The 1960s: The Height Of Change And Challenge

Defining the 1960s might be by none other than a revolution in policies, culture, and ways of human beings. The counterculture was a trend that challenged the status quo of more or less every dimension of mainstream life with its call for peace, love, liberation, and so on. A significant breakthrough in space exploration was reached on July 20th, 1969, with Neil Armstrong setting foot on the Moon, epitomizing the technological optimist ideology. Sparked by the general rights movement, the struggle for civil rights became the country's moral compass, with trailblazers like King Martin Up the threshold of equality and justice. On the other hand, music moved on, and the British invasion was responsible for the Beatles being the top seller on the pop music scene, which, in turn, influenced many generations to come.

1960s Trivia Questions

1. WHAT YEAR DID THE BEATLES FIRST APPEAR ON THE ED SULLIVAN SHOW?

   a) 1961
   b) 1962
   c) 1963
   d) 1964

2. WHICH POLITICAL FIGURE WAS ASSASSINATED IN DALLAS, TEXAS, ON NOVEMBER 22, 1963?

   a) John F. Kennedy
   b) Robert F. Kennedy
   c) Martin Luther King Jr.
   d) Malcolm X

3. WHAT CIVIL RIGHTS LEADER DELIVERED THE "I HAVE A DREAM" SPEECH IN 1963?

a) Malcolm X
b) Martin Luther King Jr.
c) Rosa Parks
d) Fred Shuttlesworth

4. WHICH 1960S TV SHOW FEATURED A SPACESHIP CALLED THE ENTERPRISE?

a) Lost in Space
b) Doctor Who
c) Star Trek
d) Battlestar Galactica

5. WHAT EVENT IN 1969 WAS DUBBED "ONE GIANT LEAP FOR MANKIND"?

a) The launch of Sputnik
b) Yuri Gagarin's orbit of the Earth
c) The Apollo 11 moon landing
d) The Apollo 13 mission

6. WHAT MUSICAL FESTIVAL HELD IN NEW YORK BECAME SYNONYMOUS
WITH THE COUNTERCULTURE MOVEMENT?

a) The Monterey Pop Festival
b) Woodstock
c) Altamont Free Concert
d) Isle of Wight Festival

7. WHAT POPULAR BRITISH SPY MOVIE SERIES, BEGINNING IN THE 1960S, FEATURED SEAN CONNERY IN THE LEAD ROLE?

a) Mission: Impossible
b) James Bond
c) Bourne Series
d) Kingsman

8. WHO WAS THE FIRST AMERICAN ASTRONAUT TO ORBIT THE EARTH IN 1962?

a) Alan Shepard
b) John Glenn
c) Gus Grissom
d) Neil Armstrong

9. WHAT U.S. SUPREME COURT DECISION LEGALIZED INTERRACIAL MARRIAGE IN 1967?

a) Brown v. Board of Education
b) Roe v. Wade
c) Loving v. Virginia
d) Miranda v. Arizona

10. WHICH 1968 STANLEY KUBRICK FILM EXPLORED SPACE EXPLORATION AND ARTIFICIAL INTELLIGENCE?

a) 2001: A Space Odyssey
b) A Clockwork Orange
c) The Shining
d) Full Metal Jacket

11. WHAT MAJOR GEOPOLITICAL EVENT BEGAN IN 1961 WITH THE CONSTRUCTION OF A DIVIDING WALL IN GERMANY?

a) The Berlin Crisis
b) The building of the Berlin Wall
c) The end of World War II
d) The fall of the Iron Curtain

12. WHICH FASHION DESIGNER POPULARIZED THE MINI-SKIRT IN THE 1960S?

a) Coco Chanel
b) Mary Quant
c) Jean Paul Gaultier
d) Vivienne Westwood

13. WHAT U.S. LEGISLATION OUTLAWED RACIAL DISCRIMINATION IN PUBLIC PLACES AND EMPLOYMENT IN 1964?

a) Voting Rights Act
b) Equal Pay Act
c) Civil Rights Act
d) Fair Housing Act

14. WHICH FOLK MUSIC GROUP POPULARIZED PROTEST SONGS LIKE "IF I HAD A HAMMER" AND "BLOWIN' IN THE WIND"?

a) The Byrds
b) Simon & Garfunkel
c) Peter, Paul and Mary
d) The Mamas & the Papas

15. WHAT MUSICAL INSTRUMENT, PLAYED BY JIMI HENDRIX, BECAME SYNONYMOUS WITH PSYCHEDELIC ROCK?

a) Drum set
b) Electric guitar
c) Keyboard
d) Bass guitar

16. WHICH 1960S ALFRED HITCHCOCK FILM BECAME FAMOUS FOR ITS SHOCKING SHOWER SCENE?

a) Vertigo
b) The Birds
c) Psycho
d) Rear Window

17. WHAT POPULAR TV VARIETY SHOW HOSTED BY JOHNNY CARSON BECAME KNOWN AS "THE KING OF LATE NIGHT"?

a) The Ed Sullivan Show
b) Saturday Night Live
c) The Tonight Show
d) The Late Show

18. WHAT FAMOUS COUPLE WAS MARRIED ON MARCH 19, 1969, IN GIBRALTAR AND SPENT THEIR HONEYMOON PROMOTING PEACE?

a) Elizabeth Taylor and Richard Burton
b) John Lennon and Yoko Ono
c) Paul McCartney and Linda Eastman
d) Mick Jagger and Bianca Pérez

19. WHAT INFLUENTIAL FEMINIST BOOK BY BETTY FRIEDAN HELPED SPARK THE WOMEN'S LIBERATION MOVEMENT?

a) The Feminine Mystique
b) Sexual Politics
c) The Second Sex
d) The Female Eunuch

20. WHICH INTERNATIONAL ATHLETIC COMPETITION IN 1968 WAS MARKED BY A POWERFUL "BLACK POWER" SALUTE BY AMERICAN ATHLETES?

a) The Rome Olympics
b) The Tokyo Olympics
c) The Mexico City Olympics
d) The Munich Olympics

21. WHICH CIVIL RIGHTS LEADER WAS AWARDED THE NOBEL PEACE PRIZE IN 1964?

a) Malcolm X
b) Rosa Parks
c) Martin Luther King Jr.
d) Fred Shuttlesworth

22. WHAT POPULAR TOY, INTRODUCED IN 1968, BECAME A MUST-HAVE FOR CHILDREN ACROSS THE U.S.?

a) Easy-Bake Oven
b) Hot Wheels
c) G.I. Joe
d) Barbie

23. WHICH COMIC BOOK SUPERHERO GROUP FIRST APPEARED IN MARVEL COMICS IN 1961?

a) The Avengers
b) X-Men
c) Fantastic Four
d) Justice League

24. WHAT BAND HEADLINED THE FIRST ROCK CONCERT AT SHEA STADIUM IN NEW YORK IN 1965?

a) The Beatles
b) The Rolling Stones
c) The Who
d) Pink Floyd

25. WHICH COUNTRY WAS INVADED BY THE SOVIET UNION AND ITS ALLIES DURING THE PRAGUE SPRING OF 1968?

a) Poland
b) Czechoslovakia
c) Hungary
d) East Germany

26. WHAT GROUNDBREAKING TV SHOW FEATURED NICHELLE NICHOLS AS ONE OF THE FIRST AFRICAN-AMERICAN WOMEN IN A PROMINENT ROLE?

a) I Spy
b) Star Trek
c) The Jeffersons
d) Julia

27. WHICH 1960S COUNTERCULTURE FILM FEATURED PETER FONDA AND DENNIS HOPPER TRAVELING ACROSS THE AMERICAN SOUTHWEST ON MOTORCYCLES?

a) Easy Rider
b) The Wild One
c) Rebel Without a Cause
d) Two-Lane Blacktop

28. WHAT U.S. PRESIDENT ANNOUNCED HIS "WAR ON POVERTY" AND THE "GREAT SOCIETY" IN THE 1960S?

a) John F. Kennedy
b) Richard Nixon
c) Lyndon B. Johnson
d) Dwight D. Eisenhower

29. WHICH BRITISH BAND BROUGHT TOGETHER MICK JAGGER AND KEITH RICHARDS, LEADING TO DECADES OF ROCK AND ROLL HITS?

a) The Beatles
b) The Rolling Stones
c) The Kinks
d) The Who

30. WHAT POPULAR PLASTIC FASHION DOLL, INTRODUCED IN 1959, BECAME A PHENOMENON IN THE 1960S?

a) Barbie
b) Tammy
c) Blythe
d) Skipper

31. WHAT CULTURAL MOVEMENT BROUGHT TOGETHER POETS AND WRITERS LIKE ALLEN GINSBERG AND Jack Kerouac in the 1960s?

a) The Beat Generation
b) The Harlem Renaissance
c) The Lost Generation
d) The Bloomsbury Group

32. WHICH FIRST LADY BECAME KNOWN FOR HER DISTINCTIVE FASHION SENSE AND REMODELING OF THE WHITE HOUSE?

a) Betty Ford
b) Jacqueline Kennedy
c) Lady Bird Johnson
d) Pat Nixon

33. WHAT BROADWAY MUSICAL ABOUT HIPPIE CULTURE, FEATURING SONGS LIKE "AQUARIUS," BECAME A HIT IN THE LATE 1960S?

a) Jesus Christ Superstar
b) Hair
c) Rent
d) The Rocky Horror Show

34. WHICH LEGENDARY ROCK BAND IS KNOWN FOR ITS 'SGT. PEPPER'S LONELY HEARTS CLUB BAND' ALBUM RELEASED IN 1967?

a) The Rolling Stones
b) The Beatles
c) The Who
d) Pink Floyd

35. WHAT PROTEST MOVEMENT OPPOSED AMERICAN INVOLVEMENT IN THE VIETNAM WAR THROUGHOUT THE 1960S?

a) Civil Rights Movement
b) Women's Liberation Movement
c) Anti-War Movement
d) Environmental Movement

36. WHICH WRITER AND ACTIVIST BECAME A PROMINENT VOICE IN THE AMERICAN CIVIL RIGHTS MOVEMENT WITH HIS BOOK 'THE FIRE NEXT TIME'?

a) James Baldwin
b) Malcolm X
c) Martin Luther King Jr.
d) Stokely Carmichael

37. WHAT FAMOUS ROCK BAND, KNOWN FOR THEIR 'WALL OF SOUND,' PERFORMED 'GOOD VIBRATIONS' AND OTHER HITS IN THE 1960S?

a) The Beach Boys
b) The Beatles
c) The Doors
d) The Rolling Stones

38. WHAT SUPERHERO TV SHOW STARRED ADAM WEST AND BURT WARD, BRINGING COMIC BOOK ACTION TO THE SMALL SCREEN?

a) Spider-Man
b) Batman
c) Superman
d) The Incredible Hulk

39. WHAT POPULAR VARIETY SHOW, KNOWN FOR ITS COMEDIC SKETCHES AND MUSIC PERFORMANCES, ENTERTAINED VIEWERS ON SATURDAY NIGHTS?

a) The Ed Sullivan Show
b) Saturday Night Live
c) The Carol Burnett Show
d) The Dean Martin Show

40. WHAT ASIAN NATION SAW AN INTENSIFICATION OF MILITARY CONFLICT DUE TO AMERICAN INVOLVEMENT IN THE 1960S?

a) Vietnam
b) Korea
c) Cambodia
d) Laos

41. WHAT ICONIC BRITISH TV SERIES DEPICTED THE ADVENTURES OF A TIME LORD AND HIS TIME-TRAVELING COMPANIONS?

a) Star Trek
b) Doctor Who
c) The Twilight Zone
d) Quantum Leap

42. WHAT WAS THE NAME OF THE SOVIET SPACECRAFT THAT FIRST REACHED THE MOON IN 1959?

a) Vostok 1
b) Sputnik 1
c) Luna 2
d) Soyuz

43. WHICH AFRICAN-AMERICAN ATHLETE BECAME FAMOUS FOR WINNING THE GOLD IN THE DECATHLON AT THE 1960 ROME OLYMPICS?

a) Jesse Owens
b) Carl Lewis
c) Rafer Johnson
d) Bob Beamon

44. WHAT ISLAND COUNTRY NEAR FLORIDA SAW A U.S.-LED INVASION ATTEMPT FAIL IN 1961?

a) Bahamas
b) Cuba
c) Puerto Rico
d) Jamaica

45. WHICH INFLUENTIAL MUSICIAN FOUNDED MOTOWN RECORDS AND LAUNCHED THE CAREERS OF SEVERAL MAJOR ARTISTS IN THE 1960S?

a) Quincy Jones
b) Berry Gordy
c) Stevie Wonder
d) Ray Charles

46. WHAT SUCCESSFUL BROADWAY MUSICAL AND FILM ADAPTATION FEATURED JULIE ANDREWS AS A GOVERNESS TO THE VON TRAPP FAMILY?

a) My Fair Lady
b) Mary Poppins
c) The Sound of Music
d) Oliver!

47. WHAT MUSIC ALBUM BY BOB DYLAN SIGNALED HIS SHIFT FROM ACOUSTIC FOLK TO ELECTRIC ROCK AND CAUSED CONTROVERSY AT THE NEWPORT FOLK FESTIVAL?

a) Blonde on Blonde
b) Highway 61 Revisited
c) Bringing It All Back Home
d) Blood on the Tracks

48. WHAT EUROPEAN POLITICAL ENTITY WAS CREATED IN THE 1960S TO FACILITATE TRADE AND ECONOMIC COOPERATION?

a) The European Union
b) The European Economic Community
c) The Eurozone
d) The Schengen Area

49. WHAT AFRICAN COUNTRY, LED BY PRESIDENT JOMO KENYATTA, GAINED INDEPENDENCE FROM BRITISH COLONIAL RULE IN THE 1960S?

a) Nigeria
b) Kenya
c) Ghana
d) Zimbabwe

50. WHAT POPULAR ANIMATED TV SERIES INTRODUCED A FAMILY LIVING IN THE FUTURE WITH A ROBOT MAID?

a) The Jetsons
b) Futurama
c) Star Trek: The Animated Series
d) Thunderbirds

51. WHICH FRENCH LEADER WITHDREW FRANCE FROM NATO AND SPEARHEADED A NEW EUROPEAN POLITICAL IDENTITY IN THE 1960S?

a) Charles de Gaulle
b) Georges Pompidou
c) François Mitterrand
d) Jacques Chirac

52. WHAT CHILDREN'S TELEVISION SHOW, INTRODUCED IN 1969, FEATURED COLORFUL CHARACTERS LIKE BIG BIRD AND COOKIE MONSTER?

a) Barney & Friends
b) Sesame Street
c) Mister Rogers' Neighborhood
d) The Magic School Bus

53. WHAT HIT SINGLE BY ARETHA FRANKLIN BECAME A RALLYING CRY FOR WOMEN AND CIVIL RIGHTS ACTIVISTS IN THE 1960S?

a) "Respect"
b) "Chain of Fools"
c) "Think"
d) "I Say a Little Prayer"

54. WHAT PUBLICATION, KNOWN FOR ITS PROVOCATIVE CONTENT, BEGAN THE "NEW JOURNALISM" MOVEMENT AND COVERED COUNTERCULTURAL ISSUES?

a) The New Yorker
b) Rolling Stone
c) Harper's Magazine
d) Life Magazine

55. WHAT AFRICAN-AMERICAN SINGER AND ACTIVIST PERFORMED "TO BE YOUNG, GIFTED AND BLACK" AND "I WISH I KNEW HOW IT WOULD FEEL TO BE FREE"?

a) Nina Simone
b) Aretha Franklin
c) Billie Holiday
d) Ella Fitzgerald

56. WHAT INNOVATIVE MUSICIAN WAS KNOWN FOR HIS FOLK SONGS THAT ADDRESSED POLITICAL AND SOCIAL ISSUES?

a) Bob Dylan
b) Neil Young
c) John Denver
d) Jim Croce

57. WHICH U.S PRESIDENT SIGNED THE MEDICARE AND MEDICAID PROGRAMS INTO LAW IN THE 1960S?

a) John F. Kennedy
b) Richard Nixon
c) Lyndon B. Johnson
d) Gerald Ford

58. WHAT EUROPEAN CITY BECAME A SYMBOL OF THE COLD WAR WHEN IT WAS DIVIDED BY A PHYSICAL BARRIER IN 1961?

a) Paris
b) Vienna
c) Berlin
d) Prague

59. WHICH JAZZ MUSICIAN RECORDED A LOVE SUPREME, ONE OF THE MOST INFLUENTIAL JAZZ ALBUMS OF THE 1960S?

a) Miles Davis
b) John Coltrane
c) Charlie Parker
d) Duke Ellington

60. WHAT WAS THE NAME OF THE COMPUTER NETWORK, FUNDED BY THE U.S GOVERNMENT, THAT BECAME THE PRECURSOR TO THE INTERNET IN THE 1960S?

a) ARPANET
b) ENIAC
c) IBM Net
d) ALTAIR Net

61. WHAT POPULAR TV SITCOM FEATURED ELIZABETH MONTGOMERY AS A MODERN-DAY WITCH LIVING WITH HER MORTAL HUSBAND?

a) I Dream of Jeannie
b) Bewitched
c) The Addams Family
d) The Munsters

62. WHAT 1960S MUSIC FESTIVAL IN THE U.K. FEATURED
PERFORMANCES BY JIMI HENDRIX, THE WHO, AND JANIS JOPLIN?

a) Glastonbury Festival
b) Reading Festival
c) Isle of Wight Festival
d) Creamfields

63. WHAT AMERICAN ARTIST IS KNOWN FOR CREATING POP
PAINTINGS OF SOUP CANS AND CELEBRITIES?

a) Roy Lichtenstein
b) Jackson Pollock
c) Andy Warhol
d) Jean-Michel Basquiat

64. WHAT ENVIRONMENTAL MOVEMENT GAINED TRACTION AFTER
RACHEL CARSON'S SILENT SPRING REVEALED THE DANGERS OF
PESTICIDES?

a) Greenpeace
b) World Wildlife Fund
c) Sierra Club
d) Earth Day

65. WHAT AMERICAN COMIC BOOK WRITER CREATED SPIDER-MAN
AND THE FANTASTIC FOUR, INTRODUCING NEW STORYTELLING
STYLES?

a) Stan Lee
b) Jack Kirby
c) Alan Moore
d) Frank Miller

66. WHAT ASIAN RELIGIOUS LEADER FLED TO INDIA IN 1959 AFTER A
FAILED UPRISING AGAINST CHINESE RULE?

a) Dalai Lama
b) Thich Nhat Hanh
c) Aung San Suu Kyi
d) Sun Yat-sen

67. WHAT AMERICAN SCI-FI AUTHOR IS KNOWN FOR WRITING STRANGER IN A STRANGE LAND AND THE MOON IS A HARSH MISTRESS?

a) Isaac Asimov
b) Arthur C. Clarke
c) Robert A. Heinlein
d) Philip K. Dick

68. WHAT EUROPEAN NATION WAS RULED BY GENERAL FRANCISCO FRANCO DURING THE 1960S?

a) Italy
b) Germany
c) Spain
d) Portugal

69. WHAT POLITICAL GROUP SOUGHT TO EMPOWER MEXICAN-AMERICAN AGRICULTURAL WORKERS IN CALIFORNIA DURING THE 1960S?

a) National Farm Workers Association
b) American Farm Bureau Federation
c) United Farm Workers
d) Workers' Rights Board

70. WHICH WELL-KNOWN ACTOR AND MARTIAL ARTIST APPEARED IN THE GREEN HORNET TV SERIES IN THE 1960S?

a) Chuck Norris
b) Bruce Lee
c) Jackie Chan
d) Jet Li

71. WHAT WAS THE NAME OF THE MASSIVE PRO-DEMOCRACY PROTESTS HELD IN PARIS, FRANCE, IN 1968?

a) May 1968 protests
b) French Revolution of 1968
c) Paris Spring
d) Bastille Day Riots

72. WHAT ORGANIZATION LED BY MALCOLM X ADVOCATED FOR BLACK SEPARATISM AND EMPOWERMENT IN THE 1960S?

a) Southern Christian Leadership Conference
b) Black Panther Party
c) Nation of Islam
d) American Civil Liberties Union

73. WHICH ROCK BAND RECORDED THE ALBUM LET IT BLEED AND TOURED EXTENSIVELY IN THE LATE 1960S?

a) The Beatles
b) The Who
c) Led Zeppelin
d) The Rolling Stones

74. WHAT FAMOUS AMUSEMENT PARK IN FLORIDA OPENED ITS DOORS TO THE PUBLIC IN THE LATE 1960S?

a) Disneyland
b) Walt Disney World
c) Universal Studios Florida
d) Busch Gardens Tampa Bay

75. WHAT WAS THE NICKNAME FOR THE MEN WHO FLEW IN NASA'S GEMINI AND APOLLO MISSIONS IN THE 1960S?

a) Flyboys
b) Space Cowboys
c) Astronauts
d) Rocket Men

76. WHICH COUNTRY ARTIST, KNOWN FOR HIS DISTINCTIVE VOICE, BECAME A LEADING FIGURE IN THE NASHVILLE SOUND DURING THE 1960S?

a) Johnny Cash
b) Willie Nelson
c) George Jones
d) Merle Haggard

77. WHAT ANTI-WAR ORGANIZATION, FOUNDED IN MICHIGAN IN THE 1960S, PROTESTED AMERICAN INVOLVEMENT IN VIETNAM?

a) Students for a Democratic Society
b) Vietnam Veterans Against the War
c) The Weather Underground
d) American Peace Mobilization

78. WHICH AFRICAN-AMERICAN ATHLETE REFUSED TO FIGHT IN THE VIETNAM WAR, CITING RELIGIOUS OBJECTIONS, AND FACED IMPRISONMENT AS A RESULT?

a) Muhammad Ali
b) Jim Brown
c) Bill Russell
d) Kareem Abdul-Jabbar

79. WHAT FAMOUS DESIGNER INTRODUCED THE "MOD" FASHION TREND IN LONDON IN THE 1960S?

a) Vivienne Westwood
b) Mary Quant
c) Paul Smith
d) Alexander McQueen

80. WHAT LANDMARK DECISION BY THE U.S. SUPREME COURT IN 1962 BANNED ORGANIZED PRAYER IN PUBLIC SCHOOLS?

a) Engel v. Vitale
b) Brown v. Board of Education
c) Roe v. Wade
d) Miranda v. Arizona

81. WHICH AMERICAN AUTHOR WON THE NOBEL PRIZE IN LITERATURE IN 1962 FOR WORKS LIKE "THE GRAPES OF WRATH" AND "EAST OF EDEN"?

a) Ernest Hemingway
b) William Faulkner
c) John Steinbeck
d) F. Scott Fitzgerald

82. WHAT WAS THE NAME OF THE CIA-SPONSORED INVASION THAT FAILED TO OVERTHROW FIDEL CASTRO'S GOVERNMENT IN 1961?

a) Bay of Pigs Invasion
b) Operation Just Cause
c) Grenada Invasion
d) Operation Anaconda

83. WHAT BROADWAY MUSICAL ABOUT A LOVABLE CONMAN BECAME A HIT ON STAGE AND LATER ON FILM IN THE 1960S?

a) Guys and Dolls
b) The Music Man
c) Oliver!
d) Fiddler on the Roo

84. WHICH COUNTRY SUCCESSFULLY TESTED ITS FIRST NUCLEAR WEAPON IN THE 1960S, BECOMING A NEW MEMBER OF THE "NUCLEAR CLUB"?

a) India
b) Israel
c) China
d) South Africa

85. WHAT MAJOR VIDEO GAME, DEVELOPED BY MIT STUDENTS IN 1962, BECAME ONE OF THE FIRST POPULAR COMPUTER GAMES?

a) Spacewar!
b) Pong
c) Asteroids
d) Pac-Man

86. WHAT EAST ASIAN COUNTRY EXPERIENCED A DRAMATIC ECONOMIC TRANSFORMATION KNOWN AS THE "MIRACLE ON THE HAN RIVER"?

a) China
b) Japan
c) South Korea
d) Vietnam

87. WHICH POPULAR AUTHOR PUBLISHED "ONE HUNDRED YEARS OF SOLITUDE" AND BECAME A LEADER OF THE "MAGICAL REALISM" LITERARY MOVEMENT?

a) Gabriel García Márquez
b) Jorge Luis Borges
c) Isabel Allende
d) Mario Vargas Llosa

88. WHAT FAMOUS SONGWRITER WROTE "TURN! TURN! TURN!" BASED ON A PASSAGE FROM THE BIBLE'S BOOK OF ECCLESIASTES?

a) Bob Dylan
b) Pete Seeger
c) Paul Simon
d) Leonard Cohen

89. WHICH ACTRESS BECAME FAMOUS FOR HER ROLE AS HOLLY GOLIGHTLY IN "BREAKFAST AT TIFFANY'S" IN THE EARLY 1960S?

a) Audrey Hepburn
b) Elizabeth Taylor
c) Marilyn Monroe
d) Grace Kelly

90. WHAT EUROPEAN CITY SAW INCREASED TOURISM AND CULTURAL SIGNIFICANCE FOLLOWING THE 1964 TOKYO SUMMER OLYMPICS?

a) Beijing
b) Seoul
c) Tokyo
d) Hong Ko

91. WHAT BRITISH BAND WAS KNOWN FOR ITS CONCEPT ALBUM "TOMMY," WHICH TOLD THE STORY OF A DEAF, DUMB, AND BLIND PINBALL WIZARD?

a) The Beatles
b) Pink Floyd
c) The Who
d) The Rolling Stones

92. WHICH POLITICAL MOVEMENT, FORMED IN THE MID-1960S, CALLED FOR INDEPENDENCE AND CULTURAL PRIDE AMONG AFRICAN NATIONS?

a) Pan-Africanism
b) Negritude
c) Afrocentrism
d) Black Power

93. WHICH COUNTRY WAS LED BY CHARLES DE GAULLE AND SAW MASSIVE STRIKES AND PROTESTS IN 1968?

a) Germany
b) France
c) Italy
d) Spain

94. WHAT CONTROVERSIAL FILM BY STANLEY KUBRICK EXPLORED THE DEHUMANIZATION OF MILITARY TRAINING AND THE VIETNAM WAR?

a) Dr. Strangelove
b) Full Metal Jacket
c) Paths of Glory
d) A Clockwork Orange

95. WHAT POPULAR SITCOM FEATURED AN IDEALIZED VERSION OF SUBURBAN AMERICAN LIFE WITH FATHER FIGURES LIKE WARD CLEAVER?

a) Leave It to Beaver
b) Father Knows Best
c) The Andy Griffith Show
d) The Dick Van Dyke Show

96. WHAT WAS THE NAME OF THE GOVERNMENT PROGRAM THAT AIMED TO PROVIDE JOBS AND TRAINING FOR DISADVANTAGED YOUTH IN THE 1960S?

a) New Deal
b) Great Society
c) Job Corps
d) Works Progress Administration

97. WHICH COUNTRY HOSTED EXPO 67, ATTRACTING MILLIONS OF VISITORS TO SHOWCASE THE LATEST IN SCIENCE AND CULTURE?

a) United States
b) France
c) Canada
d) United Kingdom

98. WHAT EUROPEAN MONARCH REMAINED IN POWER DESPITE NUMEROUS PROTESTS AND AN ASSASSINATION ATTEMPT IN THE 1960S?

a) Queen Elizabeth II
b) King Juan Carlos I
c) King Baudouin
d) Prince Rainier III

99. WHICH AMERICAN MUSICAL GROUP RELEASED THE ALBUMS "PET SOUNDS" AND "SMILE," BOTH INFLUENTIAL FOR THEIR COMPLEX HARMONIES AND ARRANGEMENTS?

a) The Beatles
b) The Beach Boys
c) The Mamas & the Papas
d) Simon & Garfunke

100. WHICH JAZZ CLUB IN NEW YORK CITY BECAME THE CENTER OF THE JAZZ REVIVAL IN THE 1960S?

a) The Blue Note
b) The Cotton Club
c) Birdland
d) The Village Vanguard

101. WHAT WAS THE NAME OF THE ANTI-CENSORSHIP LEGAL DEFENSE ORGANIZATION FORMED IN THE 1960S?

a) ACLU
b) Freedom of Expression Foundation
c) Electronic Frontier Foundation
d) Authors Guild

102. WHAT WAS THE NAME OF THE SOVIET LUNAR PROGRAM THAT SOUGHT TO BEAT THE U.S. TO THE MOON IN THE 1960S?

a) Vostok Program
b) Soyuz Program
c) Sputnik Program
d) Lunokhod Program

103. WHAT EAST AFRICAN COUNTRY SAW A MAJOR SOCIALIST EXPERIMENT UNDER PRESIDENT JULIUS NYERERE IN THE 1960S?

a) Ethiopia
b) Kenya
c) Tanzania
d) Uganda

104. WHAT AUSTRALIAN LEADER HELPED USHER IN AN ERA OF PROGRESSIVE REFORMS AND RECOGNITION FOR INDIGENOUS PEOPLE?

a) Robert Menzies
b) Gough Whitlam
c) John Howard
d) Malcolm Fraser

105. WHICH U.S. CITY SAW THE RISE OF A POWERFUL COUNTERCULTURE MUSIC SCENE CENTERED AROUND THE FILLMORE AUDITORIUM?

a) New York City
b) Los Angeles
c) San Francisco
d) Chicago

106. WHAT CHILDREN'S BOOK AUTHOR PUBLISHED "GREEN EGGS AND HAM" AND OTHER CLASSICS IN THE 1960S?

a) Roald Dahl
b) Maurice Sendak
c) Dr. Seuss
d) E.B. White

107. WHAT BRITISH PRIME MINISTER RESIGNED AMID ALLEGATIONS OF ESPIONAGE AND GOVERNMENT SCANDALS IN THE 1960S?

a) Harold Wilson
b) Edward Heath
c) Alec Douglas-Home
d) Harold Macmillan

108. WHICH SCIENTIST DEVELOPED THE CONTRACEPTIVE PILL THAT REVOLUTIONIZED WOMEN'S REPRODUCTIVE HEALTH?

a) Gregory Pincus
b) Jonas Salk
c) Alexander Fleming
d) Louis Pasteur

109. WHAT AMERICAN ROCK BAND, LED BY JIM MORRISON, BECAME FAMOUS FOR ITS DARK LYRICS AND ONSTAGE THEATRICS?

a) The Doors
b) Led Zeppelin
c) The Rolling Stones
d) Pink Floyd

110. WHICH BOOK BY MARSHALL MCLUHAN EXPLORED THE "GLOBAL VILLAGE" CONCEPT AND MEDIA'S ROLE IN SHAPING SOCIETY?

a) The Medium is the Massage
b) Understanding Media
c) The Gutenberg Galaxy
d) War and Peace in the Global Village

111. WHAT POLITICAL FIGURE WAS KNOWN FOR GIVING FIERY SPEECHES FROM A SOAPBOX IN LONDON'S HYDE PARK DURING THE 1960S?

a) Winston Churchill
b) Tony Benn
c) Enoch Powell
d) Michael Foot

112. WHAT MIDDLE EASTERN COUNTRY HOSTED THE FIRST WOMEN'S RIGHTS CONFERENCE IN 1968?

a) Iran
b) Israel
c) Lebanon
d) Turkey

113. WHAT FRENCH PHILOSOPHER LED THE STRUCTURALIST MOVEMENT AND WROTE "THE ORDER OF THINGS"?

a) Jean-Paul Sartre
b) Michel Foucault
c) Albert Camus
d) Jacques Derrida

114. WHICH CARIBBEAN ISLAND NATION WAS EXPELLED FROM THE ORGANIZATION OF AMERICAN STATES OVER ITS SOCIALIST POLICIES IN THE 1960S?

a) Cuba
b) Jamaica
c) Haiti
d) Dominican Republic

115. WHAT RELIGIOUS LEADER FAMOUSLY USED THE PHRASE "THE KINGDOM OF GOD IS WITHIN YOU" AND ADVOCATED NONVIOLENCE?

a) Pope John XXIII
b) Martin Luther King Jr.
c) Mahatma Gandhi
d) Dalai Lama

116. WHICH BESTSELLING AUTHOR PUBLISHED "TO KILL A MOCKINGBIRD" IN 1960, EXPLORING THEMES OF RACE AND JUSTICE?

a) Harper Lee
b) John Steinbeck
c) Truman Capote
d) Ralph Ellison

117. WHAT GROUP OF INDIAN MUSICIANS BECAME POPULAR IN THE U.S. AFTER COLLABORATING WITH WESTERN ROCK ARTISTS?

a) Ravi Shankar and the sitar ensemble
b) The Bollywood Brass Band
c) The Indian Raga Rockers
d) Anoushka Shankar's group

118. WHICH ACTOR AND SINGER PERFORMED "MACK THE KNIFE" AND BECAME A LEADING FIGURE IN AMERICAN JAZZ MUSIC?

a) Frank Sinatra
b) Dean Martin
c) Sammy Davis Jr.
d) Bobby Darin

119. WHAT FAMOUS WAR PHOTOGRAPHER CAPTURED THE HORRORS OF THE VIETNAM WAR FOR LIFE MAGAZINE AND OTHER PUBLICATIONS IN THE 1960S?

a) Robert Capa
b) Eddie Adams
c) Dorothea Lange
d) Nick Ut

120. WHICH AFRICAN-AMERICAN ARTIST'S "WHAT'S GOING ON" ALBUM CAPTURED THE SOCIAL AND POLITICAL MOOD OF THE 1960S?

a) James Brown
b) Marvin Gaye
c) Curtis Mayfield
d) Stevie Wonder

Answer for 1960s

1. d) 1964

2. a) John F. Kennedy

3. b) Martin Luther King Jr.

4. c) Star Trek

5. c) The Apollo 11 moon landing

6. b) Woodstock

7. b) James Bond

8. b) John Glenn

9. c) Loving v. Virginia

10. a) 2001: A Space Odyssey

11. b) The building of the Berlin Wall

12. b) Mary Quant

13. c) Civil Rights Act

14. c) Peter, Paul and Mary

15. b) Electric guitar

16. c) Psycho

17. c) The Tonight Show

18. b) John Lennon and Yoko Ono

19. a) The Feminine Mystique

20. c) The Mexico City Olympics

21. c) Martin Luther King Jr.

22. b) Hot Wheels

23. c) Fantastic Four

24. a) The Beatles

25. b) Czechoslovakia

26. b) Star Trek

27. a) Easy Rider

28. c) Lyndon B. Johnson

29. b) The Rolling Stones

30. a) Barbie

31. a) The Beat Generation

32. b) Jacqueline Kennedy

33. b) Hair

34. b) The Beatles

35. c) Anti-War Movement

36. a) James Baldwin

37. a) The Beach Boys

38. b) Batman

39. b) Saturday Night Live

40. a) Vietnam

41. b) Doctor Who

42. c) Luna 2

43. c) Rafer Johnson

44. b) Cuba

45. b) Berry Gordy

46. c) The Sound of Music

47. c) Bringing It All Back Home

48. b) The European Economic Community

49. b) Kenya

50. a) The Jetsons

51. a) Charles de Gaulle

52. b) Sesame Street

53. a) "Respect"

54. b) Rolling Stone

55. a) Nina Simone

56. a) Bob Dylan

57. c) Lyndon B. Johnson

58. c) Berlin

59. b) John Coltrane

60. a) ARPANET

61. b) Bewitched

62. c) Isle of Wight Festival

63. c) Andy Warhol

64. d) Earth Day

65. a) Stan Lee

66. a) Dalai Lama

67. c) Robert A. Heinlein

68. c) Spain

69. c) United Farm Workers

70. b) Bruce Lee

71. a) May 1968 protests

72. c) Nation of Islam

73. d) The Rolling Stones

74. b) Walt Disney World

75. c) Astronauts

76. c) George Jones

77. a) Students for a Democratic Society

78. a) Muhammad Ali

79. b) Mary Quant

80. a) Engel v. Vitale

81. c) John Steinbeck

82. a) Bay of Pigs Invasion

83. b) The Music Man

84. c) China

85. a) Spacewar!

86. c) South Korea

87. a) Gabriel García Márquez

88. b) Pete Seeger

89. a) Audrey Hepburn

90. c) Tokyo

91. c) The Who

92. a) Pan-Africanism

93. b) France

94. b) Full Metal Jacket

95. a) Leave It to Beaver

96. c) Job Corps

97. c) Canada

98. c) King Baudouin

99. b) The Beach Boys

100. d) The Village Vanguard

101. a) ACLU

102. a) Chicago

103. c) Tanzania

104. b) Gough Whitlam

105. c) San Francisco

106. c) Dr. Seuss

107. d) Harold Macmillan

108. a) Gregory Pincus

109. a) The Doors

110. b) Understanding Media

111. b) Tony Benn

112. a) Iran

113. b) Michel Foucault

114. a) Cuba

115. c) Mahatma Gandhi

116. a) Harper Lee

117. a) Ravi Shankar and the sitar ensemble

118. d) Bobby Darin

119. b) Eddie Adams

120. b) Marvin Gaye

3

The 1970s: Disco, Decadence, And Discontent

The 1970s fashion was an intricate patchwork of cultural topics and economic events. The decade's first half was stepping on the toes of the 1960s, while the latter half leaned more to the side of the change. Patrons had to reckon with the economic downturn and energy crisis that made many discos and nightclubs that dominated pop culture in that season an unimaginable dream. It was the time that saw the advent of big-budget movies such as Star Wars and The Godfather, which film lovers still remember while classic movie-making is still being redefined. Politically, despite scarred public trust, Americans have less belief and new habits in political engagement due to the Watergate scandal discounting the American institutions.

1970s Trivia Questions

1. WHICH DISCO HIT, FEATURED IN SATURDAY NIGHT FEVER, HAD EVERYONE DANCING IN THE LATE 1970S?

a) "Night Fever"
b) "Disco Inferno"
c) "Stayin' Alive"
d) "Boogie Wonderland"

2. WHAT POLITICAL SCANDAL LED TO THE RESIGNATION OF PRESIDENT RICHARD NIXON IN 1974?

a) Iran-Contra Affair
b) Watergate Scandal
c) Whitewater Controversy
d) Teapot Dome Scandal

3. WHAT MAJOR SCI-FI FILM DIRECTED BY GEORGE LUCAS BECAME A CULTURAL PHENOMENON IN 1977?

a) "Blade Runner"
b) "Star Wars"
c) "Close Encounters of the Third Kind"
d) "Alien"

4. WHO WAS THE U.S. PRESIDENT DURING THE IRAN HOSTAGE CRISIS IN 1979?

a) Jimmy Carter
b) Richard Nixon
c) Gerald Ford
d) Ronald Reagan

5. WHICH GLAM ROCK BAND, KNOWN FOR ITS OUTLANDISH COSTUMES AND FACE PAINT, ROCKED THE STAGE WITH "ROCK AND ROLL ALL NITE"?

a) Mötley Crüe
b) Kiss
c) Queen
d) Aerosmith

6. WHAT WAS THE NAME OF THE PEACE AGREEMENT SIGNED BETWEEN EGYPT AND ISRAEL IN 1978?

a) Oslo Accords
b) Camp David Accords
c) Geneva Conference
d) Dayton Agreement

7. WHICH ACTION FILM SERIES STARRING CLINT EASTWOOD AS "DIRTY" HARRY CALLAHAN GAINED POPULARITY IN THE 1970S?

a) Lethal Weapon
b) Die Hard
c) Dirty Harry
d) The French Connection

8. WHICH AMERICAN FASHION DESIGNER IS KNOWN FOR POPULARIZING WRAP DRESSES IN THE 1970S?

a) Donna Karan
b) Coco Chanel
c) Diane von Fürstenberg
d) Vera Wang

9. WHAT BROADWAY MUSICAL, ADAPTED INTO A 1978 FILM, STARRED JOHN TRAVOLTA AND OLIVIA NEWTON-JOHN AS HIGH SCHOOL SWEETHEARTS?

a) Chicago
b) West Side Story
c) Grease
d) Hairspray

10. WHAT ENVIRONMENTAL ORGANIZATION, FOUNDED IN 1971, BECAME KNOWN FOR ITS DIRECT-ACTION CAMPAIGNS?

a) Greenpeace
b) Sierra Club
c) World Wildlife Fund
d) Environmental Defense Fund

11. WHICH HISTORIC U.S. SUPREME COURT CASE IN 1973 LEGALIZED ABORTION ACROSS THE NATION?

a) Brown v. Board of Education
b) Roe v. Wade
c) Plessy v. Ferguson
d) Obergefell v. Hodges

12. WHAT MAJOR INTERNATIONAL SPORTING EVENT IN 1972 WAS MARRED BY A TRAGIC TERRORIST ATTACK?

a) The Seoul Olympics
b) The Mexico City Olympics
c) The Munich Olympics
d) The Los Angeles Olympics

13. WHICH AMERICAN ROCK BAND RELEASED THE ALBUM RUMOURS, ONE OF THE BEST-SELLING ALBUMS EVER, IN 1977?

a) The Eagles
b) Fleetwood Mac
c) The Rolling Stones
d) Led Zeppelin

14. WHAT POPULAR TV SHOW FEATURED MARY TYLER MOORE AS A SINGLE, INDEPENDENT WOMAN WORKING AT A MINNEAPOLIS NEWSROOM?

a) The Mary Tyler Moore Show
b) Murphy Brown
c) Rhoda
d) The Carol Burnett Show

15. WHICH SOUTH ASIAN COUNTRY EXPERIENCED A DEVASTATING CYCLONE IN 1970 AND A WAR OF INDEPENDENCE SHORTLY AFTER THAT?

a) India
b) Sri Lanka
c) Bangladesh
d) Pakistan

16. WHAT JAZZ-ROCK BAND POPULARIZED HITS LIKE "REELIN' IN THE YEARS" AND "RIKKI DON'T LOSE THAT NUMBER" IN THE 1970S?

a) The Doobie Brothers
b) Steely Dan
c) Chicago
d) Blood, Sweat & Tears

17. WHAT CARIBBEAN NATION GAINED INDEPENDENCE FROM THE UNITED KINGDOM IN 1973?

a) Jamaica
b) Barbados
c) Bahamas
d) Trinidad and Tobago

18. WHAT TV MINISERIES, BASED ON ALEX HALEY'S BOOK, CAPTIVATED AUDIENCES BY TRACING A FAMILY'S LINEAGE BACK TO AFRICA?

a) Roots
b) The Thorn Birds
c) Queen
d) North and South

19. WHAT SPORT GAINED GLOBAL POPULARITY WITH THE BATTLE OF THE SEXES MATCH BETWEEN BILLIE JEAN KING AND BOBBY RIGGS?

a) Tennis
b) Golf
c) Basketball
d) Table tennis

20. WHICH BROADWAY MUSICAL CENTERED AROUND THE LIVES OF DANCERS AUDITIONING FOR A SHOW?

a) Chicago
b) Cats
c) A Chorus Line
d) Les Misérables

21. WHAT VIDEO GAME FEATURING A PADDLE AND BALL BECAME ONE OF THE FIRST ARCADE HITS OF THE 1970S

a) Space Invaders
b) Asteroids
c) Pong
d) Pac-Man

22. WHICH AMERICAN COMEDIAN HOSTED THE TONIGHT SHOW FOR NEARLY THREE DECADES, BEGINNING IN THE 1970S?

a) Johnny Carson
b) Jay Leno
c) David Letterman
d) Conan O'Brien

23. WHICH SONG BY LED ZEPPELIN, NOT INITIALLY RELEASED AS A SINGLE, BECAME AN ICONIC ROCK ANTHEM OF THE 1970S?

a) "Whole Lotta Love"
b) "Black Dog"
c) "Stairway to Heaven"
d) "Kashmir"

24. WHAT AMERICAN MOVIE DIRECTOR BROUGHT AUDIENCES TO THE EDGE OF THEIR SEATS WITH HIS BLOCKBUSTER FILM JAWS IN 1975?

a) Steven Spielberg
b) George Lucas
c) Ridley Scott
d) James Cameron

25. WHICH GERMAN TERRORIST GROUP WAS RESPONSIBLE FOR A SERIES OF BOMBINGS, ASSASSINATIONS, AND KIDNAPPINGS IN THE 1970S?

a) Red Army Faction
b) Baader-Meinhof Group
c) Red Brigades
d) Action Directe

26. WHAT POPULAR TOY INTRODUCED CHILDREN TO A GALAXY FAR, FAR AWAY WITH ACTION FIGURES AND PLAYSETS?

a) G.I. Joe
b) Star Wars
c) Transformers
d) He-Man

27. WHAT LEGAL ORGANIZATION FOUNDED IN 1971 FOUGHT FOR WOMEN'S REPRODUCTIVE RIGHTS ACROSS THE U.S.?

a) American Civil Liberties Union
b) National Organization for Women
c) Planned Parenthood
d) Center for Reproductive Rights

28. WHICH U.S. PRESIDENT ISSUED A GENERAL PARDON TO VIETNAM WAR DRAFT DODGERS IN 1977?

a) Richard Nixon
b) Jimmy Carter
c) Gerald Ford
d) Ronald Reagan

29. WHAT CHILEAN PRESIDENT WAS OVERTHROWN IN A COUP D'ÉTAT LED BY GENERAL AUGUSTO PINOCHET IN 1973?

a) Salvador Allende
b) Michelle Bachelet
c) Patricio Aylwin
d) Eduardo Frei Montalva

30. WHAT CULT SCI-FI TV SERIES INTRODUCED AUDIENCES TO A FLEET OF STARSHIPS SEARCHING FOR A NEW HOME?

a) Star Trek
b) Battlestar Galactica
c) Babylon 5
d) Farscape

31. WHAT AFRICAN-AMERICAN JAZZ MUSICIAN KNOWN FOR PLAYING THE SOPRANO SAXOPHONE DIED IN 1975?

a) Charlie Parker
b) John Coltrane
c) Ornette Coleman
d) Louis Armstrong

32. WHICH AMERICAN SINGER-SONGWRITER BROUGHT THEMES OF
PROTEST AND SPIRITUALITY TO HIS ALBUMS TAPESTRY AND
SWEET BABY JAMES?

a) Bob Dylan
b) James Taylor
c) Carole King
d) Joni Mitchell

33. WHAT MAJOR POLITICAL SCANDAL, UNCOVERED BY
JOURNALISTS BOB WOODWARD AND CARL BERNSTEIN, LED TO
MULTIPLE GOVERNMENT RESIGNATIONS?

a) Iran-Contra Affair
b) Watergate Scandal
c) Lewinsky Scandal
d) Teapot Dome Scandal

34. WHAT ASIAN COUNTRY WAS REUNIFIED IN 1975 AFTER DECADES
OF WAR AND OCCUPATION BY FOREIGN POWERS?

a) Korea
b) Vietnam
c) Cambodia
d) Laos

35. WHICH CARIBBEAN NATION, KNOWN FOR ITS REGGAE MUSIC AND
RASTAFARIAN CULTURE, GAINED INDEPENDENCE IN 1976?

a) Jamaica
b) Haiti
c) Cuba
d) Trinidad and Tobago

36. WHICH AMERICAN BOXER WON THE HEAVYWEIGHT TITLE BY
DEFEATING GEORGE FOREMAN IN THE "RUMBLE IN THE JUNGLE"
IN 1974?

a) Muhammad Ali
b) Joe Frazier
c) Mike Tyson
d) Evander Holyfield

37. WHAT TECHNOLOGICAL INNOVATION BROUGHT HIGH-FIDELITY SOUND TO MUSIC LOVERS AND AUDIOPHILES IN THE 1970S?

a) 8-track tape
b) Compact disc
c) Vinyl record
d) Cassette tape

38. WHICH BEST-SELLING AUTHOR WROTE CARRIE AND THE SHINING, HELPING TO DEFINE MODERN HORROR LITERATURE?

a) Stephen King
b) Dean Koontz
c) Clive Barker
d) Peter Straub

39. WHICH ITALIAN FILM DIRECTOR WON ACCLAIM FOR HIS 1970 MOVIE THE CONFORMIST, WHICH EXAMINED POLITICS AND MORALITY?

a) Federico Fellini
b) Bernardo Bertolucci
c) Michelangelo Antonioni
d) Roberto Rossellini

40. WHAT MIDDLE EASTERN ORGANIZATION WAS FORMED IN 1970 TO REPRESENT THE INTERESTS OF THE PALESTINIAN PEOPLE?

a) Arab League
b) Hezbollah
c) Hamas
d) Palestine Liberation Organization

41. WHAT NETWORK OF SECRET INFORMANTS COLLABORATED WITH THE STASI, EAST GERMANY'S INTELLIGENCE AGENCY, THROUGHOUT THE 1970S?

a) KGB Network
b) CIA Network
c) Inoffizielle Mitarbeiter
d) Volkspolizei

42. WHICH ASIAN GOVERNMENT IMPLEMENTED THE "ONE CHILD POLICY" IN THE LATE 1970S TO CONTROL POPULATION GROWTH?

a) Japan
b) South Korea
c) Vietnam
d) China

43. WHAT AFRICAN COUNTRY, LED BY IDI AMIN, WAS KNOWN FOR ITS BRUTAL REGIME AND HUMAN RIGHTS ABUSES IN THE 1970S?

a) Nigeria
b) Uganda
c) Rwanda
d) Zimbabwe

44. WHICH EASTERN EUROPEAN NATION BECAME KNOWN FOR ITS "PRAGUE SPRING" OF POLITICAL AND SOCIAL REFORMS IN 1968?

a) Poland
b) Czechoslovakia
c) Hungary
d) Yugoslavia

45. WHAT POLITICAL LEADER ESTABLISHED AN AUTHORITARIAN REGIME IN INDONESIA DURING THE "NEW ORDER" ERA?

a) Sukarno
b) Suharto
c) B.J. Habibie
d) Megawati Sukarnoputri

46. WHICH BRITISH ROCK BAND INTRODUCED THE WORLD TO SONGS LIKE "BOHEMIAN RHAPSODY" AND "WE WILL ROCK YOU" IN THE 1970S?

a) The Beatles
b) Led Zeppelin
c) Queen
d) Pink Floyd

47. WHAT CENTRAL AMERICAN COUNTRY ENDURED A CIVIL WAR BETWEEN LEFTIST GUERRILLAS AND GOVERNMENT FORCES FROM 1979 ONWARD?

a) Panama
b) Nicaragua
c) El Salvador
d) Honduras

48. WHICH AMERICAN TV SERIES BROUGHT COMEDY AND COMMENTARY ABOUT THE KOREAN WAR INTO PEOPLE'S HOMES IN THE 1970S?

a) The Vietnam War
b) MASH
c) The Cold War
d) Tour of Duty

49. WHAT BRITISH AUTHOR BECAME A MAJOR FIGURE IN THE FANTASY GENRE WITH HER SERIES ABOUT A MAGICAL BOARDING SCHOOL?

a) J.K. Rowling
b) Diana Wynne Jones
c) Ursula K. Le Guin
d) Margaret Atwood

50. WHAT TV DRAMA CHRONICLED THE LIVES OF A FAMILY LIVING IN RURAL VIRGINIA DURING THE GREAT DEPRESSION AND WORLD WAR II?

a) The Waltons
b) Little House on the Prairie
c) Bonanza
d) The Thorn Birds

51. WHICH AMERICAN JAZZ MUSICIAN BROUGHT A FUSION OF JAZZ, FUNK, AND R&B TO A WIDER AUDIENCE WITH HEADHUNTERS IN 1973?

a) Miles Davis
b) John Coltrane
c) Herbie Hancock
d) Louis Armstrong

52. WHAT VIDEO GAME FEATURING A YELLOW CHARACTER EATING DOTS BECAME A WORLDWIDE ARCADE SENSATION IN THE LATE 1970S?

a) Space Invaders
b) Pong
c) Pac-Man
d) Tetris

53. WHAT EUROPEAN NATION EXPERIENCED A SOCIALIST REVOLUTION IN 1974 THAT OUSTED A LONG-STANDING DICTATORSHIP?

a) Spain
b) Portugal
c) Italy
d) Greece

54. WHICH AMERICAN TENNIS PLAYER WON THE GRAND SLAM OF ALL FOUR MAJOR TENNIS TOURNAMENTS IN 1972?

a) Andre Agassi
b) Pete Sampras
c) Billie Jean King
d) Rod Laver

55. WHAT AMERICAN CITY BECAME KNOWN FOR ITS "SILICON VALLEY" DUE TO THE RISE OF HIGH-TECH COMPANIES IN THE 1970S?

a) Los Angeles
b) San Francisco
c) San Jose
d) Seattle

56. WHICH AFRICAN-AMERICAN SINGER-SONGWRITER RELEASED THE ALBUMS TALKING BOOK AND SONGS IN THE KEY OF LIFE IN THE 1970S?

a) Marvin Gaye
b) Stevie Wonder
c) James Brown
d) Michael Jackson

57. AFTER YEARS OF CONFLICT, WHAT AFRICAN COUNTRY GAINED INDEPENDENCE FROM PORTUGUESE COLONIAL RULE IN 1975?

a) Angola
b) Mozambique
c) South Africa
d) Zimbabwe

58. WHICH POLITICAL LEADER WON THE NOBEL PEACE PRIZE IN 1971 FOR PROMOTING DEMOCRACY AND HUMAN RIGHTS IN THE AMERICAS?

a) Nelson Mandela
b) Jimmy Carter
c) Oscar Arias Sanchez
d) Henry Kissinger

59. WHAT AMERICAN NEWSPAPER BECAME FAMOUS FOR UNCOVERING THE WATERGATE SCANDAL IN THE 1970S?

a) The New York Times
b) The Washington Post
c) The Los Angeles Times
d) USA Today

60. WHICH 1970S ANIMATED TV SERIES, CREATED BY HANNA-BARBERA, FEATURED A FUTURISTIC FAMILY LIVING IN ORBIT CITY?

a) The Flintstones
b) The Jetsons
c) Scooby-Doo
d) Thundercats

61. WHICH INDIAN PRIME MINISTER DECLARED A STATE OF EMERGENCY IN 1975, SUSPENDING CIVIL LIBERTIES AND IMPRISONING OPPONENTS?

a) Rajiv Gandhi
b) Lal Bahadur Shastri
c) Indira Gandhi
d) Atal Bihari Vajpayee

62. WHAT JAPANESE CAR MANUFACTURER BECAME KNOWN FOR ITS COMPACT, FUEL-EFFICIENT VEHICLES THAT BECAME POPULAR IN THE U.S.?

a) Suzuki
b) Mitsubishi
c) Toyota
d) Honda

63. WHICH AMERICAN FOLK ROCK BAND RELEASED ALBUMS LIKE DÉJÀ VU AND CROSBY, STILLS & NASH IN THE 1970S?

a) The Eagles
b) Crosby, Stills, Nash & Young
c) Fleetwood Mac
d) The Byrds

64. WHAT WAS THE NAME OF THE U.S. ECONOMIC POLICY THAT ATTEMPTED TO CURB INFLATION AND STIMULATE GROWTH IN THE 1970S?

a) New Deal
b) Reaganomics
c) Ford's WIN (Whip Inflation Now)
d) Johnson's Great Society

65. WHICH MEXICAN-AMERICAN CIVIL RIGHTS LEADER FOUGHT FOR FARMWORKERS' RIGHTS AND ORGANIZED THE UNITED FARM WORKERS?

a) Dolores Huerta
b) Cesar Chavez
c) Antonio Villaraigosa
d) Rodolfo Gonzales

66. WHAT FILM INTRODUCED THE WORLD TO AN EPIC LOVE STORY ABOARD AN ILL-FATED OCEAN LINER?

a) Titanic
b) The Poseidon Adventure
c) A Night to Remember
d) The Love Boat

67. WHICH POPULAR AMERICAN JAZZ MUSICIAN AND BANDLEADER WON A GRAMMY AWARD FOR HIS ALBUM FUTURE SHOCK IN 1976?

a) Miles Davis
b) Duke Ellington
c) Herbie Hancock
d) John Coltrane

68. WHAT FAMOUS ANIMATED TV SHOW INTRODUCED CHILDREN TO A TALKING DOG AND HIS FRIENDS SOLVING MYSTERIES IN THE 1970S?

a) Tom and Jerry
b) Scooby-Doo, Where Are You!
c) The Pink Panther Show
d) Looney Tunes

69. WHAT WAS THE NAME OF THE POLITICAL PARTY LED BY MARGARET THATCHER THAT WON THE U.K. GENERAL ELECTION IN 1979?

a) Labour Party
b) Conservative Party
c) Liberal Democrats
d) UK Independence Party

70. WHICH ISRAELI PRIME MINISTER WAS AWARDED THE NOBEL PEACE PRIZE FOR SIGNING A PEACE TREATY WITH EGYPT IN THE 1970S?

a) Yitzhak Rabin
b) Menachem Begin
c) Shimon Peres
d) Benjamin Netanyahu

71. WHAT AMERICAN COMEDIAN RELEASED RICHARD PRYOR: LIVE IN CONCERT, ONE OF THE FIRST CONCERT FILMS, IN 1979?

a) Eddie Murphy
b) George Carlin
c) Richard Pryor
d) Bill Cosby

72. WHICH MIDDLE EASTERN COUNTRY UNDERWENT AN ISLAMIC REVOLUTION IN 1979 THAT ESTABLISHED A NEW THEOCRATIC GOVERNMENT?

a) Saudi Arabia
b) Iran
c) Iraq
d) Afghanistan

73. WHAT COMPUTER MANUFACTURER WAS FOUNDED BY STEVE JOBS AND STEVE WOZNIAK IN 1976, LAUNCHING THE PERSONAL COMPUTER ERA?

a) IBM
b) Apple Inc.
c) Microsoft
d) Dell

74. WHICH SOUTH AMERICAN COUNTRY EXPERIENCED A MILITARY COUP IN 1976 THAT OUSTED ISABEL PERÓN FROM POWER?

a) Brazil
b) Argentina
c) Chile
d) Peru

75. WHICH LATIN AMERICAN AUTHOR WROTE ONE HUNDRED YEARS OF SOLITUDE, A LANDMARK WORK IN MAGICAL REALISM?

a) Isabel Allende
b) Jorge Luis Borges
c) Gabriel García Márquez
d) Mario Vargas Llosa

76. WHAT AMERICAN ACTION FILM SERIES STARRING CHARLES BRONSON AS A VIGILANTE BROUGHT VIOLENCE AND RETRIBUTION TO THE SCREEN?

a) Lethal Weapon
b) Die Hard
c) Dirty Harry
d) Death Wish

77. WHICH EUROPEAN NATION IMPLEMENTED A GENEROUS
WELFARE STATE AND PROGRESSIVE SOCIAL REFORMS IN THE
1970S?

a) United Kingdom
b) Sweden
c) Germany
d) France

78. WHAT EUROPEAN ISLAND NATION GAINED INDEPENDENCE FROM
BRITISH COLONIAL RULE IN 1974 AND JOINED THE UNITED
NATIONS?

a) Iceland
b) Malta
c) Cyprus
d) Ireland

79. WHICH JAZZ MUSICIAN'S ALBUM, HEAD HUNTERS, BROKE NEW
GROUND BY FUSING JAZZ WITH FUNK AND SOUL IN THE 1970S?

a) Miles Davis
b) Charles Mingus
c) Herbie Hancock
d) John Coltrane

80. WHAT WAS THE NAME OF THE ROCK BAND FORMED BY
BROTHERS ANGUS AND MALCOLM YOUNG THAT BECAME A
HEAVY METAL SENSATION?

a) Metallica
b) Black Sabbath
c) AC/DC
d) Led Zeppelin

81. WHICH AMERICAN AUTHOR EXPLORED THE WATERGATE SCANDAL AND THE PENTAGON PAPERS IN ALL THE PRESIDENT'S MEN?

a) Stephen King
b) Bob Woodward
c) Hunter S. Thompson
d) Norman Mailer

82. WHAT MIDDLE EASTERN COUNTRY WAS CREATED IN 1971, BRINGING TOGETHER SEVERAL EMIRATES TO FORM A NEW FEDERATION?

a) Saudi Arabia
b) Qatar
c) Bahrain
d) United Arab Emirates

83. WHAT SPORT BECAME MORE ACCESSIBLE WITH THE DEVELOPMENT OF NEW LIGHTWEIGHT FIBERGLASS AND GRAPHITE EQUIPMENT IN THE 1970S?

a) Basketball
b) Soccer
c) Tennis
d) Golf

84. WHICH EUROPEAN LEADER HELPED ESTABLISH THE EUROPEAN ECONOMIC COMMUNITY AND CHAMPIONED EUROPEAN UNITY?

a) Margaret Thatcher
b) François Mitterrand
c) Helmut Schmidt
d) Charles de Gaulle

85. WHAT INDIAN CITY BECAME KNOWN AS A SOFTWARE DEVELOPMENT AND OUTSOURCING CENTER IN THE 1970S?

a) Mumbai
b) Bangalore
c) New Delhi
d) Hyderabad

86. WHAT POPULAR TV VARIETY SHOW ENTERTAINED VIEWERS
WITH COMEDY SKETCHES, MUSIC, AND CELEBRITY GUESTS IN
THE 1970S?

a) The Ed Sullivan Show
b) The Carol Burnett Show
c) Saturday Night Live
d) The Muppet Show

87. WHICH GERMAN FILM DIRECTOR EXPLORED THE DARK SIDE OF
HUMAN NATURE IN HIS 1979 FILM THE TIN DRUM?

a) Werner Herzog
b) Rainer Werner Fassbinder
c) Volker Schlöndorff
d) Wim Wenders

88. WHAT WAS THE NAME OF THE ECONOMIC POLICY IMPLEMENTED
BY THE U.K. GOVERNMENT THAT LED TO THE "WINTER OF
DISCONTENT"?

a) Thatcherism
b) Blairism
c) Keynesian economics
d) Monetarism

89. WHICH CENTRAL AMERICAN NATION WAS RULED BY THE
SOMOZA FAMILY DICTATORSHIP BEFORE A SOCIALIST
REVOLUTION IN THE 1970S?

a) Guatemala
b) El Salvador
c) Nicaragua
d) Honduras

90. WHAT AMERICAN MUSICIAN RELEASED ALBUMS LIKE SONGS IN
THE KEY OF LIFE AND INNERVISIONS, DEFINING THE SOUND OF
THE 1970S?

a) Marvin Gaye
b) Stevie Wonder
c) Al Green
d) Curtis Mayfield

91. WHICH AFRICAN LEADER LED HIS COUNTRY TO INDEPENDENCE AND ADVOCATED SOCIALIST REFORMS IN THE 1970S?

a) Kwame Nkrumah
b) Julius Nyerere
c) Nelson Mandela
d) Jomo Kenyatta

92. WHAT JAPANESE ELECTRONICS COMPANY BECAME KNOWN FOR ITS HIGH-QUALITY AUDIO EQUIPMENT AND TELEVISIONS IN THE 1970S?

a) Toshiba
b) Sony
c) Panasonic
d) Sharp

93. WHICH SCIENCE FICTION TV SHOW INTRODUCED A NEW GENERATION TO THE ADVENTURES OF CAPTAIN KIRK AND MR. SPOCK IN THE 1970S?

a) Star Trek: The Original Series
b) Star Trek: The Next Generation
c) Battlestar Galactica
d) Doctor Who

94. WHAT TECHNOLOGICAL INNOVATION ALLOWED BUSINESSES TO STORE LARGE AMOUNTS OF DATA ON MAGNETIC TAPE DRIVES IN THE 1970S?

a) Floppy disks
b) Hard disk drives
c) Magnetic tape storage
d) Optical disk

95. WHICH AMERICAN SCIENTIST IS KNOWN FOR POPULARIZING THE GAIA HYPOTHESIS, WHICH VIEWS EARTH AS A SELF-REGULATING ORGANISM?
a) Carl Sagan
b) Richard Dawkins
c) James Lovelock
d) Stephen Hawking

96. WHAT ENVIRONMENTAL ORGANIZATION PUBLISHED THE REPORT LIMITS TO GROWTH, WARNING ABOUT THE EFFECTS OF OVERPOPULATION?

a) Greenpeace
b) Sierra Club
c) World Wildlife Fund
d) Club of Rome

97. WHICH BRITISH PRIME MINISTER SUPPORTED THE FORMATION OF THE EUROPEAN COMMUNITY AND IMPROVED RELATIONS WITH THE U.S.?

a) Harold Wilson
b) Edward Heath
c) Margaret Thatcher
d) Tony Blair

98. WHAT FAMOUS FRENCH FASHION DESIGNER POPULARIZED THE "LE SMOKING" TUXEDO SUIT FOR WOMEN IN THE 1970S?

a) Christian Dior
b) Coco Chanel
c) Yves Saint Laurent
d) Pierre Cardin

99. WHAT BEST-SELLING BOOK BY RICHARD DAWKINS INTRODUCED THE CONCEPT OF "SELFISH GENES" AND EVOLUTIONARY BIOLOGY IN THE 1970S?

a) The Blind Watchmaker
b) The Selfish Gene
c) The Extended Phenotype
d) Climbing Mount Improbable

100. WHICH AMERICAN FEMINIST LEADER CO-FOUNDED THE
NATIONAL ORGANIZATION FOR WOMEN AND FOUGHT FOR
GENDER EQUALITY?

a) Gloria Steinem
b) Betty Friedan
c) Angela Davis
d) Germaine Greer

101. WHAT AFRICAN-AMERICAN ATHLETE BROKE RACIAL BARRIERS
IN TENNIS AND BECAME THE FIRST BLACK MAN TO WIN
WIMBLEDON IN 1975?

a) Arthur Ashe
b) Althea Gibson
c) Yannick Noah
d) James Blake

102. WHAT MIDDLE EASTERN POLITICAL GROUP WAS KNOWN FOR ITS
ARMED RESISTANCE AGAINST ISRAELI OCCUPATION IN THE
1970S?

a) Al-Qaeda
b) Hamas
c) Hezbollah
d) Palestine Liberation Organization (PLO)

103. WHICH EUROPEAN COUNTRY EXPANDED ITS INFLUENCE IN
AFRICA AND THE MIDDLE EAST THROUGH ITS OIL INDUSTRY IN
THE 1970S?

a) Italy
b) United Kingdom
c) France
d) Netherlands

104. WHAT ASIAN COUNTRY EXPERIENCED RAPID ECONOMIC
GROWTH UNDER THE RULE OF GENERAL PARK CHUNG-HEE IN
THE 1970S?

a) Japan
b) South Korea
c) China
d) Vietnam

105. WHAT AMERICAN ROCK BAND RELEASED THE ALBUMS DARK SIDE OF THE MOON AND WISH YOU WERE HERE IN THE 1970S?

a) The Beatles
b) Led Zeppelin
c) Pink Floyd
d) The Rolling Stones

106. WHICH SOUTH AFRICAN POLITICAL LEADER LED THE ANTI-APARTHEID STRUGGLE AND WON THE NOBEL PEACE PRIZE IN THE 1970S?

a) Nelson Mandela
b) Desmond Tutu
c) Oliver Tambo
d) Albertina Sisulu

107. WHAT U.S. STATE BECAME A CENTER FOR HIGH-TECH INNOVATION DUE TO ITS RESEARCH UNIVERSITIES AND VENTURE CAPITAL IN THE 1970S?

a) Texas
b) Massachusetts
c) California
d) New York

108. WHICH AFRICAN-AMERICAN POET PUBLISHED FOR COLORED GIRLS WHO HAVE CONSIDERED SUICIDE/WHEN THE RAINBOW IS ENUF IN 1975?

a) Maya Angelou
b) Toni Morrison
c) Ntozake Shange
d) Alice Walker

109. WHAT AFRICAN NATION UNDERWENT A SOCIALIST REVOLUTION
AND ALLIED WITH THE SOVIET UNION IN THE 1970S?

a) Ethiopia
b) Angola
c) Zimbabwe
d) Mozambique

110. WHICH BRITISH BAND RELEASED ALBUMS LIKE HOUSES OF THE
HOLY AND PHYSICAL GRAFFITI, BECOMING A LEADING FORCE IN
ROCK?

a) The Beatles
b) The Who
c) Led Zeppelin
d) Queen

111. WHAT SOVIET LEADER BECAME KNOWN FOR HIS POLICY OF
DÉTENTE AND ATTEMPTS TO IMPROVE RELATIONS WITH THE U.S.
IN THE 1970S?

a) Nikita Khrushchev
b) Leonid Brezhnev
c) Yuri Andropov
d) Mikhail Gorbachev

112. WHAT ASIAN NATION EMERGED AS A REGIONAL POWER AFTER
WINNING THE INDO-PAKISTANI WAR OF 1971?

a) India
b) Pakistan
c) Bangladesh
d) Nepal

113. WHICH FRENCH FILMMAKER EXPLORED THE MEANING OF ART
AND HISTORY IN HIS 1973 FILM DAY FOR NIGHT?

a) Jean-Luc Godard
b) François Truffaut
c) Jacques Tati
d) Louis Malle

114. WHAT AMERICAN AUTHOR WROTE HELTER SKELTER, DETAILING THE CRIMES COMMITTED BY THE MANSON FAMILY IN THE 1970S?

a) Truman Capote
b) Norman Mailer
c) Vincent Bugliosi
d) Hunter S. Thompson

115. WHICH CENTRAL AMERICAN COUNTRY SAW A LEFTIST GOVERNMENT RISE TO POWER AFTER OVERTHROWING THE MILITARY JUNTA IN 1979?

a) Guatemala
b) El Salvador
c) Nicaragua
d) Honduras

116. WHAT POLITICAL MOVEMENT IN NORTHERN IRELAND SOUGHT TO END BRITISH RULE AND UNIFY IRELAND IN THE 1970S?

a) Sinn Féin
b) Irish Republican Army (IRA)
c) Ulster Volunteer Force
d) Democratic Unionist Party

117. WHICH BRITISH POP STAR RELEASED THE ALBUMS GOODBYE YELLOW BRICK ROAD AND CAPTAIN FANTASTIC IN THE 1970S?
a) David Bowie
b) Rod Stewart
c) Elton John
d) Paul McCartney

118. WHAT WAS THE NAME OF THE SOVIET SPACE STATION THAT ORBITED EARTH FROM 1971 TO 1986?

a) Mir
b) Salyut
c) Skylab
d) Sputnik

119. WHICH ASIAN NATION WAS KNOWN FOR ITS RED GUARDS AND
THE CULTURAL REVOLUTION, WHICH SOUGHT TO RESHAPE
SOCIETY?

a) Vietnam
b) China
c) North Korea
d) Cambodia

120. WHAT AMERICAN COMEDIAN CREATED THE FIRST STAND-UP
COMEDY SPECIAL TO AIR ON CABLE TV IN THE LATE 1970S?

a) Richard Pryor
b) George Carlin
c) Robin Williams
d) Bill Cosby

1970s Answers

1. c) "Stayin' Alive"

2. a) Watergate Scandal

3. b) Star Wars

4. a) Jimmy Carter

5. b) KISS

6. b) Camp David Accords

7. c) Dirty Harry

8. c) Diane von Fürstenberg

9. c) Grease

10. c) Greenpeace

11. b) Roe v. Wade

12. c) Munich Olympics

13. b) Fleetwood Mac

14. a) The Mary Tyler Moore Show

15. c) Bangladesh

16. b) Steely Dan

17. c) Bahamas

18. a) Roots

19. a) Tennis

20. c) A Chorus Line

21. c) Pong

22. a) Johnny Carson

23. c) "Stairway to Heaven"

24. a) Steven Spielberg

25. a) Red Army Faction

26. b) Star Wars

27. d) Center for Reproductive Rights

28. b) Jimmy Carter

29. b) Salvador Allende

30. b) Battlestar Galactica

31. b) John Coltrane

32. b) James Taylor

33. b) Watergate Scandal

34. b) Vietnam

35. a) Jamaica

36. a) Muhammad Ali

37. c) Vinyl record

38. a) Stephen King

39. b) Bernardo Bertolucci

40. d) Palestine Liberation Organization

41. c) Inoffizielle Mitarbeiter

42. b) China

43. b) Uganda

44. b) Czechoslovakia

45. b) Suharto

46. c) Queen

47. c) El Salvador

48. b) MASH

49. a) J.K. Rowling

50. a) The Waltons

51. c) Herbie Hancock

52. c) Pac-Man

53. b) Portugal

54. d) Rod Laver

55. c) San Jose

56. b) Stevie Wonder

57. b) Mozambique

58. d) Henry Kissinger

59. b) The Washington Post

60. b) The Jetsons

61. c) Indira Gandhi

62. d) Honda

63. b) Crosby, Stills, Nash & Young

64. c) Ford's WIN (Whip Inflation Now)

65. b) Cesar Chavez

66. a) Titanic

67. c) Herbie Hancock

68. b) Scooby-Doo, Where Are You!

69. b) Conservative Party

70. b) Menachem Begin

71. c) Richard Pryor

72. b) Iran

73. b) Apple Inc.

74. b) Argentina

75. c) Gabriel García Márquez

76. d) Death Wish

77. b) Sweden

78. b) Malta

79. c) Herbie Hancock

80. c) AC/DC

81. b) Bob Woodward

82. d) United Arab Emirates

83. c) Tennis

84. d) Charles de Gaulle

85. b) Bangalore

86. b) The Carol Burnett Show

87. c) Volker Schlöndorff

88. d) Monetarism

89. b) Nicaragua

90. b) Stevie Wonder

91. b) Julius Nyerere

92. b) Sony

93. b) Star Trek: The Next Generation

94. c) Magnetic tape storage

95. c) James Lovelock

96. d) Club of Rome

97. b) Edward Heath

98. c) Yves Saint Laurent

99. b) The Selfish Gene

100. b) Betty Friedan

101. a) Arthur Ashe

102. d) Palestine Liberation Organization (PLO)

103. c) France

104. b) South Korea

105. c) Pink Floyd

106. b) Desmond Tutu

107. c) California

108. c) Ntozake Shange

109. b) Angola

110. c) Led Zeppelin

111. b) Leonid Brezhnev

112. a) India

113. b) François Truffaut

114. c) Vincent Bugliosi

115. c) Nicaragua

116. b) Irish Republican Army (IRA)

117. c) Elton John

118. b) Salyut

119. b) China

120. b) George Carlin

4

The 1980s: An Explosion of Media and Technology

The 80s has seen many important things resonate in the form of technological changes, basically in communications development. Personal computers caused a disruption of the revolution being used by people as they worked with their new technology, while on the other hand, MTV came up and changed the music industry by means of music videos, which became instrumental in the fame of a certain artist. On the economic level, Reagan and Thatcher were supposed to be fearless market supporters. The term Cold War symbolized a period of tension between two major powers when the threat of direct and armed clashes seemed imminent. Yet, its ice stalemate started to break and finally brought it to its peaceful end as the decade was about to end also markedly by the fall of the Berlin Wall in 1989.

1980s Trivia Questions

1. WHAT ICONIC MUSIC VIDEO BY MICHAEL JACKSON FEATURED ZOMBIES DANCING TO "THRILLER"?

   a) Ghosts
   b) Beat It
   c) Thriller
   d) Bad

2. WHICH 1984 COMEDY INTRODUCED AUDIENCES TO A TEAM OF SCIENTISTS BATTLING SUPERNATURAL CREATURES?

   a) Airplane!
   b) Police Academy
   c) Ghostbusters
   d) Scrooged

3. WHAT ACTION MOVIE FEATURED BRUCE WILLIS AS DETECTIVE JOHN MCCLANE IN A LOS ANGELES SKYSCRAPER?

   a) Lethal Weapon
   b) Die Hard
   c) Predator
   d) RoboCop

4. WHICH FAMOUS POP SINGER EARNED THE NICKNAME "MATERIAL GIRL" DURING THE 1980S?

a) Cyndi Lauper
b) Whitney Houston
c) Madonna
d) Tina Turner

5. WHICH BRITISH ROCK BAND WAS KNOWN FOR HITS LIKE "RADIO GA GA" AND "UNDER PRESSURE"?

a) The Rolling Stones
b) Queen
c) Pink Floyd
d) The Who

6. WHAT MUSIC NETWORK REVOLUTIONIZED HOW PEOPLE CONSUMED MUSIC VIDEOS IN THE EARLY 1980S?

a) ABC
b) MTV
c) VH1
d) CBS

7. WHICH ANIMATED TV SERIES FOLLOWED THE ADVENTURES OF A YOUNG BOY NAMED HE-MAN IN A MYTHICAL WORLD?

a) ThunderCats
b) The Smurfs
c) He-Man and the Masters of the Universe
d) Transformers

8. WHICH AMERICAN FILM DIRECTOR BECAME FAMOUS FOR BLOCKBUSTER HITS LIKE E.T. AND INDIANA JONES?

a) George Lucas
b) Steven Spielberg
c) James Cameron
d) Ridley Scott

9. WHAT JAPANESE VIDEO GAME COMPANY LAUNCHED THE NINTENDO ENTERTAINMENT SYSTEM IN THE MID-1980S?

a) Sony
b) Sega
c) Nintendo
d) Atari

10. WHICH MUSIC GENRE ORIGINATED IN THE BRONX AND BROUGHT RAPPING, DJING, BREAKDANCING, AND GRAFFITI ART TO THE MAINSTREAM?

a) Rock
b) Jazz
c) Hip-Hop
d) Pop

11. WHAT ANIMATED TV SERIES FEATURED A ROBOTIC CAT FROM THE FUTURE THAT HELPED A YOUNG BOY NAVIGATE EVERYDAY CHALLENGES?

a) Astro Boy
b) Doraemon
c) Pokémon
d) Dragon Ball

12. WHAT 1986 NUCLEAR DISASTER BECAME ONE OF THE WORST ACCIDENTS IN HISTORY, AFFECTING MILLIONS IN EUROPE?

a) Three Mile Island
b) Fukushima
c) Chornobyl
d) Hiroshima

13. WHICH BRITISH PRIME MINISTER WAS NICKNAMED THE "IRON LADY" DUE TO HER POLITICAL TOUGHNESS IN THE 1980S?

a) Margaret Thatcher
b) Tony Blair
c) John Major
d) Elizabeth II

14. WHAT COUNTRY MUSIC GROUP RELEASED THE ALBUM MOUNTAIN MUSIC AND BECAME ONE OF THE BEST-SELLING COUNTRY ACTS?

a) The Eagles
b) Alabama
c) Dixie Chicks
d) Brooks & Dunn

15. WHAT 1980S ARCADE GAME FEATURED A YELLOW CHARACTER NAVIGATING A MAZE AND EATING PELLETS WHILE AVOIDING GHOSTS?

a) Space Invaders
b) Tetris
c) Pac-Man
d) Super Mario Bros.

16. WHAT AMERICAN ROCK BAND RELEASED THE ALBUM THE JOSHUA TREE, BLENDING ROCK WITH SOCIAL COMMENTARY?

a) Metallica
b) U2
c) Guns N' Roses
d) Aerosmith

17. WHICH 1980S FILM FRANCHISE STARRED MICHAEL J. FOX TRAVELING THROUGH TIME IN A DELOREAN?

a) Star Wars
b) Back to the Future
c) The Terminator
d) Blade Runner

18. WHAT 1980S SATURDAY MORNING CARTOON INTRODUCED AUDIENCES TO GIANT ROBOTS THAT COULD TRANSFORM INTO VEHICLES?

a) Voltron
b) The Transformers
c) G.I. Joe
d) ThunderCats

19. WHICH BRITISH NEW WAVE BAND PERFORMED HITS LIKE "HUNGRY LIKE THE WOLF" AND "RIO"?

a) The Cure
b) Depeche Mode
c) Duran Duran
d) The Smiths

20. WHICH AFRICAN-AMERICAN COMEDIAN MADE AUDIENCES LAUGH WITH HIS STAND-UP COMEDY SPECIAL DELIRIOUS?

a) Chris Rock
b) Eddie Murphy
c) Richard Pryor
d) Bill Cosby

21. WHAT AMERICAN TV SITCOM STARRED BILL COSBY AS DR. CLIFF HUXTABLE, A SUCCESSFUL DOCTOR RAISING A FAMILY?

a) Family Ties
b) Full House
c) The Cosby Show
d) Cheers

22. WHICH DANCE WORKOUT VIDEO FEATURING JANE FONDA BECAME ONE OF THE BEST-SELLING EXERCISE PROGRAMS OF THE 1980S?

a) Jazzercise
b) Buns of Steel
c) Jane Fonda's Workout
d) The Richard Simmons Show

23. WHAT INTERNATIONAL SPORTING EVENT WAS HELD IN LOS ANGELES IN 1984, BOYCOTTED BY THE SOVIET UNION AND ITS ALLIES?

a) The Winter Olympics
b) The FIFA World Cup
c) The Summer Olympics
d) The Commonwealth Games

24. WHICH ICONIC ITALIAN FASHION DESIGNER WAS TRAGICALLY MURDERED OUTSIDE HIS HOME IN 1997?

   a) Giorgio Armani
   b) Donatella Versace
   c) Gianni Versace
   d) Roberto Cavalli

25. WHAT WAS THE NETWORK'S NAME THAT AIRED MIAMI VICE, KNIGHT RIDER, AND OTHER ACTION SHOWS IN THE 1980S?

   a) CBS
   b) NBC
   c) ABC
   d) FOX

26. WHICH AMERICAN PRESIDENT, FAMOUS FOR HIS "STAR WARS" MISSILE DEFENSE SYSTEM, LED THE U.S. THROUGH MOST OF THE 1980S?

   a) Jimmy Carter
   b) Ronald Reagan
   c) George H.W. Bush
   d) Bill Clinton

27. WHAT MIDDLE EASTERN ORGANIZATION WAS FOUNDED IN 1987 AND LED THE FIRST PALESTINIAN UPRISING AGAINST ISRAEL?

   a) PLO
   b) Hamas
   c) Hezbollah
   d) ISIS

28. WHICH 1982 ALBUM BY MICHAEL JACKSON BECAME THE BEST-SELLING ALBUM OF ALL TIME?

   a) Bad
   b) Thriller
   c) Off the Wall
   d) Dangerous

29. WHAT AMERICAN ANIMATED TV SERIES FOLLOWED THE ADVENTURES OF FOUR ANTHROPOMORPHIC TURTLES FIGHTING CRIME IN NEW YORK?

a) Teenage Mutant Ninja Turtles
b) Gargoyles
c) ThunderCats
d) The Powerpuff Girls

30. WHICH ASIAN ELECTRONICS MANUFACTURER LAUNCHED THE WALKMAN, ALLOWING PEOPLE TO LISTEN TO CASSETTE TAPES ON THE GO?

a) Samsung
b) Sony
c) Panasonic
d) Toshiba

31. WHAT ANIMATED DISNEY FILM INTRODUCED AUDIENCES TO SIMBA, A LION CUB DESTINED TO BECOME KING OF THE SAVANNA?

a) Aladdin
b) The Jungle Book
c) The Lion King
d) Bambi

32. WHICH 1988 ACTION COMEDY BROUGHT EDDIE MURPHY TO THE FICTIONAL AFRICAN KINGDOM OF ZAMUNDA?

a) Trading Places
b) Beverly Hills Cop
c) Coming to America
d) 48 Hrs

33. WHICH COUNTRY, LED BY MIKHAIL GORBACHEV, IMPLEMENTED POLICIES LIKE GLASNOST AND PERESTROIKA IN THE LATE 1980S?

a) China
b) Russia
c) East Germany
d) The Soviet Union

34. WHAT POPULAR BOARD GAME CHALLENGED PLAYERS TO NAVIGATE LIFE'S "UPS AND DOWNS" WHILE AVOIDING BANKRUPTCY?

a) Monopoly
b) Life
c) Payday
d) Risk

35. WHICH 1985 FANTASY ADVENTURE MOVIE FEATURED A YOUNG SEAN ASTIN SEARCHING FOR TREASURE WITH A GROUP OF MISFIT FRIENDS?

a) The Goonies
b) E.T. the Extra-Terrestrial
c) Labyrinth
d) Stand By Me

36. WHAT 1986 ANIMATED FILM DEPICTED THE CONFLICT BETWEEN AUTOBOTS AND DECEPTICONS IN A BATTLE FOR CONTROL OF THE UNIVERSE?

a) Voltron
b) Transformers: The Movie
c) Robotech
d) He-Man

37. WHAT POPULAR TOY LINE INTRODUCED A SERIES OF CUSTOMIZABLE PLASTIC BRICKS THAT COULD BE USED TO BUILD ELABORATE STRUCTURES?

a) K'NEX
b) LEGO
c) Mega Bloks
d) Lincoln Logs

38. WHICH AMERICAN SOAP OPERA EXPLORED THE LIVES OF THE WEALTHY EWING FAMILY AND THEIR OIL BUSINESS?

a) Falcon Crest
b) Dallas
c) Dynasty
d) Knots Landing

39. WHAT MIDDLE EASTERN TERRORIST GROUP GAINED INFAMY BY HIJACKING AIRPLANES AND KIDNAPPING WESTERNERS IN THE 1980S?

a) Al-Qaeda
b) ISIS
c) Hezbollah
d) Hamas

40. WHICH AMERICAN SINGER-SONGWRITER BECAME KNOWN FOR HIS RASPY VOICE AND SONGS LIKE "BORN IN THE USA"?

a) Bruce Springsteen
b) Bob Dylan
c) Billy Joel
d) Tom Petty

41. WHICH VIDEO GAME CONSOLE INTRODUCED PLAYERS TO MARIO, ZELDA, AND OTHER CLASSIC CHARACTERS?

a) Sega Genesis
b) Atari 2600
c) Nintendo Entertainment System (NES)
d) PlayStation

42. WHAT ANIMATED T.V. SERIES FEATURED THE MISADVENTURES OF THE SMURFS LIVING IN THEIR MAGICAL VILLAGE?

a) The Flintstones
b) The Smurfs
c) Care Bears
d) My Little Pony

43. WHAT ICONIC FASHION ACCESSORY BECAME SYNONYMOUS WITH HIGH-END ELEGANCE AND CHIC STYLE IN THE 1980S?

a) Leather jackets
b) Ray-Ban sunglasses
c) Swatch watches
d) Leg warmers

44. WHICH AMERICAN POP STAR BECAME KNOWN FOR HIS "KING OF POP" TITLE, EXTRAVAGANT OUTFITS, AND SIGNATURE DANCE MOVES?

a) Prince
b) Michael Jackson
c) Madonna
d) David Bowi

45. WHAT JAPANESE ANIMATED SERIES FEATURED GIANT ROBOTS COMBINING TO FIGHT EVIL ACROSS THE GALAXY?

a) Gundam
b) Voltron
c) Macross
d) Transformers

46. WHICH AMERICAN T.V. SITCOM FOLLOWED A GROUP OF YOUNG FRIENDS NAVIGATING LIFE IN A FICTIONAL HIGH SCHOOL IN CALIFORNIA?

a) Beverly Hills, 90210
b) Saved by the Bell
c) The Fresh Prince of Bel-Air
d) Full House

47. WHAT 1980S SCI-FI FRANCHISE FEATURED A CREW ON A STARSHIP EXPLORING THE UNIVERSE UNDER THE COMMAND OF CAPTAIN PICARD?

a) Battlestar Galactica
b) Star Wars
c) Star Trek: The Next Generation
d) Babylon 5

48. WHICH FAMOUS AFRICAN-AMERICAN TALK SHOW HOST LAUNCHED HER HIGHLY SUCCESSFUL DAYTIME TALK SHOW IN 1986?

a) Whoopi Goldberg
b) Oprah Winfrey
c) Tyra Banks
d) Wendy Williams

49. WHAT FAMOUS FITNESS INSTRUCTOR ENCOURAGED VIEWERS TO "SWEAT TO THE OLDIES" WITH HIS POPULAR AEROBIC WORKOUTS?

a) Billy Blanks
b) Richard Simmons
c) Jane Fonda
d) Tony Horton

50. WHICH 1984 ROCK MOCKUMENTARY BY ROB REINER SATIRIZED THE EXCESSES OF HEAVY METAL BANDS ON TOUR?

a) Rock Star
b) This Is Spinal Tap
c) Almost Famous
d) The Rocker

51. WHAT TOY LINE BY MATTEL INTRODUCED A MAGICAL WORLD OF FAIRIES, UNICORNS, AND SORCERERS THAT YOUNG GIRLS ADORED?

a) My Little Pony
b) Cabbage Patch Kids
c) Barbie
d) She-Ra: Princess of Power

52. WHICH 1980S COMPUTER SYSTEM REVOLUTIONIZED HOME COMPUTING WITH ITS COLORFUL GRAPHICS AND USER-FRIENDLY INTERFACE?

a) IBM PC
b) Apple Macintosh
c) Commodore 64
d) Atari ST

53. WHICH AMERICAN ROCK BAND BECAME FAMOUS FOR THEIR SONGS "EVERY BREATH YOU TAKE" AND "ROXANNE"?

   a) Aerosmith
   b) The Police
   c) U2
   d) Guns N' Roses

54. WHAT 1980S ARCADE GAME REQUIRED PLAYERS TO GUIDE A FROG ACROSS A BUSY ROAD AND A RIVER TO REACH ITS HOME?

   a) Pac-Man
   b) Space Invaders
   c) Frogger
   d) Donkey Kong

55. WHICH AMERICAN T.V. SHOW FEATURED DAVID HASSELHOFF AND A TALKING CAR NAMED KITT FIGHTING CRIME TOGETHER?

   a) Miami Vice
   b) Knight Rider
   c) The A-Team
   d) MacGyver

56. WHAT COLORFUL DOLLS, KNOWN FOR THEIR DISTINCTIVE TUFT OF HAIR AND CHEERFUL EXPRESSIONS, BECAME A 1980S CRAZE?

   a) Barbie
   b) Rainbow Brite
   c) Care Bears
   d) Troll doll

57. WHICH BRITISH PRIME MINISTER LED THE NATION THROUGH ECONOMIC CHANGES AND THE FALKLANDS WAR?

   a) Winston Churchill
   b) Margaret Thatcher
   c) Tony Blair
   d) John Major

58. WHICH AMERICAN ACTOR BECAME A POP CULTURE ICON, SUCH AS INDIANA JONES AND HAN SOLO, IN THE 1980S?

a) Tom Cruise
b) Harrison Ford
c) Bruce Willis
d) Arnold Schwarzenegger

59. WHICH AMERICAN T.V. NETWORK LAUNCHED THE REAL WORLD, A REALITY SHOW THAT SET THE STAGE FOR FUTURE REALITY PROGRAMMING?

a) NBC
b) CBS
c) ABC
d) MTV

60. WHICH JAPANESE TECH COMPANY RELEASED THE GAME BOY IN 1989, REVOLUTIONIZING PORTABLE GAMING?

a) Sony
b) Nintendo
c) Sega
d) Panasonic

61. WHICH ACTION FILM STARRING ARNOLD SCHWARZENEGGER AS A CYBERNETIC ASSASSIN WAS RELEASED IN 1984?

a) Die Hard
b) Commando
c) The Terminator
d) Predator

62. WHAT SOVIET LEADER WORKED WITH THE U.S. TO REDUCE NUCLEAR ARMS AND EASE COLD WAR TENSIONS IN THE LATE 1980S?

a) Leonid Brezhnev
b) Mikhail Gorbachev
c) Yuri Andropov
d) Boris Yeltsin

63. WHICH AMERICAN COMEDY SERIES STARRED ROSEANNE BARR AS A WORKING-CLASS MOTHER RAISING HER FAMILY IN THE MIDWEST?

a) Full House
b) Roseanne
c) Married with Children
d) The Cosby Show

64. WHAT MAJOR CORPORATE SCANDAL IN THE LATE 1980S INVOLVED JUNK BONDS AND INSIDER TRADING BY FINANCIERS?

a) Enron scandal
b) Savings and Loan crisis
c) Black Monday
d) Watergate scandal

65. WHICH RAP GROUP BROUGHT HIP-HOP TO THE MASSES WITH POLITICALLY CHARGED LYRICS AND HITS LIKE "FIGHT THE POWER"?

a) N.W.A
b) Public Enemy
c) Run-D.M.C.
d) Beastie Boys

66. WHAT AMERICAN CITY EXPERIENCED A MAJOR TECH BOOM DUE TO THE RAPID GROWTH OF THE COMPUTER INDUSTRY IN THE 1980S?

a) Chicago
b) New York City
c) Silicon Valley
d) Seattle

67. WHICH AMERICAN TENNIS PLAYER EARNED THE NICKNAME "SUPERBRAT" FOR HIS ON-COURT TEMPER TANTRUMS IN THE 1980S?

a) Andre Agassi
b) John McEnroe
c) Pete Sampras
d) Jimmy Connors

68. WHAT 1989 ANIMATED T.V. SHOW, CREATED BY MATT GROENING, SATIRIZED AMERICAN LIFE WITH THE ADVENTURES OF HOMER, MARGE, BART, AND LISA?

a) Family Guy
b) South Park
c) The Simpsons
d) King of the Hill

69. WHICH AMERICAN ACTOR PLAYED "FERRIS BUELLER," THE CLEVER HIGH SCHOOL STUDENT WHO SKIPPED SCHOOL FOR A FUN DAY IN CHICAGO?

a) Matthew Broderick
b) Michael J. Fox
c) John Cusack
d) Tom Hanks

70. WHAT COMPUTER MANUFACTURER BECAME KNOWN FOR ITS "THINK DIFFERENT" CAMPAIGN AND COLORFUL IMACS IN THE LATE 1980S?

a) IBM
b) Microsoft
c) Apple
d) Dell

71. WHICH POLITICAL GROUP LAUNCHED A SERIES OF TERRORIST ATTACKS IN NORTHERN IRELAND THROUGHOUT THE 1980S?

a) IRA (Irish Republican Army)
b) ETA (Basque Homeland and Freedom)
c) Red Brigades
d) PLO (Palestine Liberation Organization)

72. WHICH AMERICAN T.V. SERIES FOLLOWED THE ANTICS OF FOUR WOMEN LIVING TOGETHER IN MIAMI, FLORIDA?

a) Designing Women
b) The Golden Girls
c) Sex and the City
d) Friends

73. WHAT 1984 AMERICAN HORROR MOVIE INTRODUCED AUDIENCES TO FREDDY KRUEGER, A VENGEFUL SPIRIT ATTACKING TEENAGERS IN THEIR DREAMS?

a) Friday the 13th
b) A Nightmare on Elm Street
c) Halloween
d) Poltergeist

74. WHICH AMERICAN T.V. NETWORK BROADCASTS SATURDAY NIGHT LIVE, CHEERS, AND OTHER HIT SHOWS?

a) ABC
b) CBS
c) NBC
d) FOX

75. WHAT 1980S ARCADE GAME FEATURED A PLUMBER JUMPING THROUGH LEVELS TO RESCUE PRINCESS TOADSTOOL FROM AN EVIL VILLAIN?

a) Pac-Man
b) Donkey Kong
c) Super Mario Bros.
d) Sonic the Hedgehog

76. WHICH AMERICAN SITCOM STARRED MICHAEL J. FOX AS A TEENAGE CONSERVATIVE WHO BUTTED HEADS WITH HIS LIBERAL PARENTS?

a) Growing Pains
b) Family Ties
c) Full House
d) The Wonder Years

77. WHAT ICONIC WHITE SNEAKERS BECAME A POPULAR FASHION STATEMENT THANKS TO HIP-HOP ARTISTS AND BASKETBALL PLAYERS?

a) Converse All-Stars
b) Nike Air Jordans
c) Adidas Superstar
d) Reebok Pumps

78. WHICH AMERICAN T.V. SHOW BOB BARKER HOSTED BECAME A DAYTIME TELEVISION STAPLE WITH ITS GAMES AND PRIZES?

a) Wheel of Fortune
b) The Price Is Right
c) Let's Make a Deal
d) Jeopardy!

79. WHAT JAPANESE COMPANY BECAME A LEADER IN HOME ELECTRONICS WITH ITS PORTABLE CASSETTE PLAYERS AND HIGH-FIDELITY STEREOS?

a) Panasonic
b) Sony
c) Toshiba
d) Hitachi

80. WHICH AMERICAN T.V. SERIES FEATURED YOUNG FBI AGENTS MULDER AND SCULLY INVESTIGATING PARANORMAL PHENOMENA?

a) The X-Files
b) The Twilight Zone
c) Buffy the Vampire Slayer
d) Twin Peaks

81. WHAT RAP GROUP RELEASED THE ALBUM LICENSED TO ILL, BLENDING ROCK AND HIP-HOP WITH HITS LIKE "NO SLEEP TILL BROOKLYN"?

a) N.W.A
b) Public Enemy
c) Beastie Boys
d) Run-D.M.C.

82. WHICH AMERICAN CITY EXPERIENCED A MAJOR ECONOMIC DECLINE DUE TO THE STEEL INDUSTRY'S COLLAPSE IN THE 1980S?

a) Detroit
b) Pittsburgh
c) Cleveland
d) Chicago

83. WHICH AMERICAN MUSIC GROUP BECAME KNOWN FOR THEIR ELABORATE STAGE SHOWS, BLENDING ROCK, FUNK, AND R&B?

a) Earth, Wind & Fire
b) KISS
c) Pink Floyd
d) Parliament-Funkadelic

84. WHAT EUROPEAN POP DUO BECAME FAMOUS FOR THEIR CATCHY TUNES BEFORE THEIR LIP-SYNCING SCANDAL WAS EXPOSED?

a) Wham!
b) Milli Vanilli
c) ABBA
d) Roxette

85. WHAT TOY CRAZE INVOLVED COLORFUL PLUSH ANIMALS WITH PLASTIC TAGS THAT BECAME VALUABLE COLLECTOR'S ITEMS IN THE LATE 1980S?

a) Cabbage Patch Kids
b) Beanie Babies
c) Furbies
d) My Little Pony

86. WHICH FASHION TREND SAW PEOPLE WEARING OVERSIZED BLAZERS WITH PADDED SHOULDERS AND BRIGHTLY COLORED LEGGINGS?

a) Punk
b) Disco
c) Grunge
d) New Wave

87. WHICH AMERICAN ACTOR AND COMEDIAN STARRED IN MOVIES LIKE TRADING PLACES AND COMING TO AMERICA?

a) Eddie Murphy
b) Bill Murray
c) Robin Williams
d) Dan Aykroyd

88. WHAT 1982 SCI-FI MOVIE BY RIDLEY SCOTT EXPLORED A DYSTOPIAN FUTURE WITH REPLICANTS AND CYBERNETIC HUMANS?

a) The Terminator
b) Blade Runner
c) Total Recall
d) Tron

89. WHICH AMERICAN ROCK BAND PERFORMED HITS LIKE "SWEET CHILD OF MINE" AND "WELCOME TO THE JUNGLE"?

a) Aerosmith
b) Guns N' Roses
c) AC/DC
d) Metallica

90. WHICH AMERICAN FITNESS ICON PROMOTED A HEALTHY LIFESTYLE THROUGH HIS BRIGHT OUTFITS AND ENERGETIC AEROBICS ROUTINES?

a) Billy Blanks
b) Richard Simmons
c) Jake Steinfeld
d) Tony Little

91. WHAT FASHION TREND SAW YOUNG PEOPLE WEARING COLORFUL BRACELETS, T-SHIRTS, AND PARACHUTE PANTS?

a) Hip Hop
b) Punk
c) Disco
d) New Wav

92. WHICH SCI-FI MOVIE SERIES INTRODUCED AUDIENCES TO RIPLEY, A SPACE EXPLORER BATTLING DEADLY EXTRATERRESTRIAL CREATURES?

a) Star Wars
b) Alien
c) Star Trek
d) Predator

93. WHAT ASIAN COUNTRY EXPERIENCED RAPID INDUSTRIALIZATION DUE TO GOVERNMENT POLICIES AND FOREIGN INVESTMENT IN THE 1980S?

a) China
b) Japan
c) South Korea
d) India

94. WHICH AMERICAN ROCK BAND RELEASED SLIPPERY WHEN WET, A DEFINING ALBUM OF THE GLAM ROCK ERA?
a) Mötley Crüe
b) Bon Jovi
c) Def Leppard
d) Poison

95. WHICH AMERICAN TENNIS PLAYER BECAME FAMOUS FOR HIS POWERFUL SERVE AND RIVALRY WITH JOHN MCENROE IN THE 1980S?

a) Andre Agassi
b) Pete Sampras
c) Ivan Lendl
d) Jimmy Connors

96. WHAT TECH COMPANY RELEASED THE COMMODORE 64, ONE OF THE BEST-SELLING HOME COMPUTERS OF THE 1980S?

a) Apple
b) IBM
c) Commodore
d) Microsoft

97. WHICH AMERICAN SCI-FI AUTHOR EXPLORED THE CONCEPT OF VIRTUAL REALITY AND CYBERNETIC ENHANCEMENTS IN HIS BOOK NEUROMANCER?

a) Philip K. Dick
b) Isaac Asimov
c) William Gibson
d) Arthur C. Clarke

98. WHICH POP MUSIC GROUP BECAME A SENSATION WITH THEIR SYNCHRONIZED DANCE MOVES AND HITS LIKE "BYE BYE BYE"?

a) New Kids on the Block
b) Backstreet Boys
c) NSYNC
d) Boyz II Men

99. WHAT TOY LINE INTRODUCED TRANSFORMING ROBOTS THAT COULD CHANGE INTO VEHICLES, ANIMALS, AND WEAPONS?

a) LEGO
b) Transformers
c) He-Man
d) G.I. Joe

100. WHICH AMERICAN ROCK BAND RELEASED APPETITE FOR DESTRUCTION, BLENDING HEAVY METAL WITH PUNK ROCK?

a) Metallica
b) Guns N' Roses
c) AC/DC
d) Nirvana

101. WHICH BRITISH AUTHOR PUBLISHED MIDNIGHT'S CHILDREN, EXPLORING THE POST-COLONIAL HISTORY OF INDIA?

a) Salman Rushdie
b) V.S. Naipaul
c) J.K. Rowling
d) Ian McEwan

102. WHICH AMERICAN JAZZ MUSICIAN RELEASED TUTU, BLENDING JAZZ WITH FUNK AND ELECTRONIC MUSIC?

a) Miles Davis
b) John Coltrane
c) Herbie Hancock
d) Charlie Parker

103. WHAT EUROPEAN FASHION DESIGNER BECAME FAMOUS FOR HIS BOLD COLORS, GEOMETRIC PATTERNS, AND FUTURISTIC DESIGNS?

a) Giorgio Armani
b) Jean Paul Gaultier
c) Versace
d) Karl Lagerfeld

104. WHICH AMERICAN ATHLETE SET THE WORLD RECORD IN THE 100-METER DASH AT THE 1988 SEOUL OLYMPICS?

a) Carl Lewis
b) Michael Johnson
c) Usain Bolt
d) Ben Johnson

105. WHAT RAP DUO BECAME FAMOUS FOR THEIR HUMOROUS RHYMES AND DANCE MOVES IN THE 1980S?

a) Run-D.M.C.
b) Beastie Boys
c) Salt-N-Pepa
d) Kid 'n Play

106. WHICH TOY CRAZE HAD KIDS COLLECTING AND TRADING COLORFUL PLASTIC CARDS REPRESENTING DIFFERENT MONSTER CHARACTERS?

a) Pokémon
b) Garbage Pail Kids
c) Cabbage Patch Kids
d) Monster in My Pocket

107. WHICH AMERICAN ANIMATED T.V. SERIES INTRODUCED AUDIENCES TO A FAMILY OF YELLOW CHARACTERS LIVING IN SPRINGFIELD?

a) Family Guy
b) The Simpsons
c) South Park
d) King of the Hill

108. WHICH BRITISH BAND PERFORMED "DO THEY KNOW IT'S CHRISTMAS?" TO RAISE MONEY FOR FAMINE RELIEF IN AFRICA?

a) The Beatles
b) Band Aid
c) Queen
d) Pink Floyd

109. WHAT WAS THE NAME OF THE 1988 DISNEY FILM THAT MIXED LIVE-ACTION WITH ANIMATION AND FEATURED ROGER RABBIT AND JESSICA RABBIT?

a) Who Framed Roger Rabbit
b) Cool World
c) Space Jam
d) Looney Tunes: Back in Action

110. WHICH EUROPEAN NATION BECAME A MEMBER OF THE EUROPEAN COMMUNITY IN THE 1980S AFTER YEARS OF DICTATORSHIP?

a) Spain
b) Portugal
c) Greece
d) Poland

1980s

1. c) Thriller

2. c) Ghostbusters

3. b) Die Hard

4. c) Madonna

5. b) Queen

6. b) MTV

7. c) He-Man and the Masters of the Universe

8. b) Steven Spielberg

9. c) Nintendo

10. c) Hip hop

11. b) Doraemon

12. c) Chernobyl

13. a) Margaret Thatcher

14. b) Alabama

15. c) "Pac-Man"

16. b) U2

17. b) Back to the Future

18. b) Transformers

19. c) Duran Duran

20. b) Eddie Murphy

21. c) The Cosby Show

22. d) Jane Fonda's Workout

23. c) The Summer Olympics

24. a) Gianni Versace

25. b) NBC

26. d) Ronald Reagan

27. b) Hamas

28. b) Thriller

29. a) Teenage Mutant Ninja Turtles

30. b) Sony

31. c) The Lion King

32. c) Coming to America

33. d) The Soviet Union

34. b) Life

35. a) The Goonies

36. b) Transformers: The Movie

37. b) LEGO

38. b) "Dallas"

39. c) Hezbollah

40. a) Bruce Springsteen

41. c) Nintendo Entertainment System (NES)

42. b) The Smurfs

43. b) Ray-Ban sunglasses

44. b) Michael Jackson

45. b) Voltron

46. a) Saved by the Bell

47. c) Star Trek: The Next Generation

48. b) Oprah Winfrey

49. b) Richard Simmons

50. b) This Is Spinal Tap

51. d) She-Ra: Princess of Power

52. b) Apple Macintosh

53. b) The Police

54. c) Frogger

55. b) Knight Rider

56. d) Troll dolls

57. b) Margaret Thatcher

58. b) Harrison Ford

59. d) MTV

60. b) Nintendo

61. c) The Terminator

62. b) Mikhail Gorbachev

63. b) Roseanne

64. b) Savings and Loan crisis

65. b) Public Enemy

66. c) Silicon Valley

67. b) John McEnroe

68. c) The Simpsons

69. a) Matthew Broderick

70. c) Apple

71. b) IRA (Irish Republican Army)

72. b) The Golden Girls

73. b) A Nightmare on Elm Street

74. c) NBC

75. c) Super Mario Bros

76. b) Family Ties

77. c) Adidas Superstar

78. b) The Price Is Right

79. b) Sony

80. a) The X-Files

81. c) Beastie Boys

82. b) Pittsburgh

83. a) Earth, Wind & Fire

84. b) Milli Vanilli

85. b) Beanie Babies

86. d) New Wave

87. a) Eddie Murphy

88. b) Blade Runner

89. b) Guns N' Roses

90. b) Richard Simmons

91. a) Hip Hop

92. b) Alien

93. c) South Korea

94. b) Bon Jovi

95. d) Jimmy Connors

96. c) Commodore

97. c) William Gibson

98. c) NSYNC

99. b) Transformers

100. b) Guns N' Roses

101. a) Salman Rushdie

102. a) Miles Davis

103. b) Jean Paul Gaultier

104. d) Ben Johnson

105. d) Kid 'n Play

106. b) Garbage Pail Kids

107. b) The Simpsons

108. b) Band Aid

109. a) Who Framed Roger Rabbit

110. a) Spain

5

The 1990s: The Digital Dawn

The 1990s were dominated by the digital revolution. The Internet emerged as a new frontier, fundamentally changing communication, entertainment, and commerce. The cultural landscape was as vibrant as ever, with grunge and hip-hop redefining the music scene. Pop culture phenomena like Harry Potter and The Matrix influenced a new generation. On the global stage, the decade saw significant changes such as the dissolution of the Soviet Union early on and the deepening of globalization, impacting economies and cultures around the world.

1990s Trivia Questions

1. WHAT BRITISH BAND RELEASED THE ALBUM "MORNING GLORY" (WHAT'S THE STORY) IN 1995, FEATURING HITS LIKE "WONDERWALL"?

   a) Blur
   b) Pulp
   c) The Verve
   d) Oasis

2. WHICH 1993 SCI-FI MOVIE, DIRECTED BY STEVEN SPIELBERG, FEATURED DINOSAURS BROUGHT BACK TO LIFE USING DNA?

   a) Jurassic Park
   b) Jurassic world
   c) The Lost World
   d) Dinosaur

3. WHAT T.V. SHOW FOLLOWED SIX FRIENDS NAVIGATING LIFE IN NEW YORK CITY, MAKING "THE RACHEL" HAIRCUT A 1990S FASHION STAPLE?

   a) Seinfeld
   b) Friends
   c) Mad About You
   d) Living Single

4. WHICH AMERICAN RAP ARTIST BECAME KNOWN FOR HITS LIKE "CALIFORNIA LOVE" AND HIS INVOLVEMENT IN THE EAST COAST-WEST COAST RIVALRY?

a) Snoop Dogg
b) Notorious B.I.G.
c) Tupac Shakur
d) Jay-Z

5. WHAT FIRST-PERSON SHOOTER GAME, RELEASED IN 1996, POPULARIZED ONLINE MULTIPLAYER GAMING WITH ITS "DEATHMATCH" MODE?

a) Doom
b) Quake
c) Duke Nukem 3D
d) Half-Life

6. WHICH ANIMATED DISNEY FILM INTRODUCED AUDIENCES TO THE ADVENTURES OF ALADDIN, A STREET THIEF IN THE FICTIONAL CITY OF AGRABAH?

a) The Lion King
b) Aladdin
c) Mulan
d) Hercules

7. WHAT JAPANESE GAMING CONSOLE, RELEASED IN 1994, BECAME A GLOBAL SENSATION WITH ITS CD-ROM-BASED GAMES?

a) Nintendo 64
b) Sega Saturn
c) Sony PlayStation
d) Panasonic 3DO

8. WHICH AFRICAN-AMERICAN TALK SHOW HOST BECAME KNOWN FOR HER BOOK CLUB AND HIGH-PROFILE CELEBRITY INTERVIEWS IN THE 1990S?

a) Oprah Winfrey
b) Queen Latifah
c) Tyra Banks
d) Whoopi Goldberg

9. WHICH T.V. DRAMA SERIES FEATURED DAVID DUCHOVNY AND GILLIAN ANDERSON AS FBI AGENTS INVESTIGATING PARANORMAL PHENOMENA?

a) The Outer Limits
b) The X-Files
c) Stranger Things
d) Fringe

10. WHAT ANIMATED T.V. SHOW FEATURED THE ADVENTURES OF THREE SISTERS WITH SUPERPOWERS FIGHTING EVIL IN TOWNSVILLE?

a) The Magic School Bus
b) The Powerpuff Girls
c) Totally Spies
d) Sailor Moon

11. WHAT 1997 JAMES CAMERON FILM, SET ABOARD AN ILL-FATED OCEAN LINER, BECAME ONE OF THE HIGHEST-GROSSING FILMS OF ALL TIME?

a) Titanic
b) Avatar
c) The Poseidon Adventure
d) Water world

12. WHAT SPORTS EVENT IN ATLANTA, GEORGIA, WAS MARRED BY A TRAGIC BOMBING ATTACK IN 1996?

a) The Super Bowl
b) The Summer Olympics
c) The Masters Tournament
d) The World Series

13. WHICH AMERICAN BOY BAND PERFORMED HITS LIKE "I WANT IT THAT WAY" AND "QUIT PLAYING GAMES (WITH MY HEART)"?

a) NSYNC
b) Backstreet Boys
c) New Kids on the Block
d) 98 Degrees

14. WHAT BRITISH AUTHOR BECAME A LITERARY SENSATION WITH HER HARRY POTTER SERIES ABOUT A YOUNG WIZARD?

a) J.R.R. Tolkien
b) J.K. Rowling
c) Roald Dahl
d) Neil Gaiman

15. WHAT ONLINE MARKETPLACE, LAUNCHED IN 1995, BECAME ONE OF THE LARGEST E-COMMERCE PLATFORMS FOR BUYING AND SELLING GOODS?

a) Alibaba
b) eBay
c) Etsy
d) Amazon

16. WHICH AMERICAN T.V. SHOW FEATURED THE LIVES OF A GROUP OF HIGH SCHOOL STUDENTS LED BY ZACH MORRIS IN CALIFORNIA?

a) Beverly Hills, 90210
b) Saved by the Bell
c) Dawson's Creek
d) The Fresh Prince of Bel-Air

17. WHAT ANIMATED T.V. SHOW CREATED BY MIKE JUDGE FOLLOWED TWO TEENAGE METALHEADS WREAKING HAVOC IN THEIR NEIGHBORHOOD?

a) South Park
b) Beavis and Butt-Head
c) King of the Hill
d) Daria

18. WHICH AMERICAN PRESIDENT, KNOWN FOR PLAYING THE SAXOPHONE ON LATE-NIGHT T.V., SERVED TWO TERMS IN THE 1990S?

a) George H.W. Bush
b) Bill Clinton
c) Jimmy Carter
d) Ronald Reagan

19. WHICH AMERICAN SINGER BECAME AN INTERNATIONAL
    SENSATION WITH HER BABY ONE MORE TIME ALBUM?

    a) Mariah Carey
    b) Britney Spears
    c) Jessica Simpson
    d) Christina Aguilera

20. WHAT MAJOR TECH COMPANY RELEASED THE WINDOWS 95
    OPERATING SYSTEM, POPULARIZING THE START BUTTON AND
    TASKBAR?

    a) Apple
    b) Microsoft
    c) Dell
    d) IBM

21. WHICH AMERICAN SITCOM FEATURED A STAND-UP COMEDIAN
    AND HIS FRIENDS NAVIGATING THE QUIRKS OF EVERYDAY LIFE IN
    NEW YORK?

    a) Friends
    b) Seinfeld
    c) Cheers
    d) Frasier

22. WHAT INTERNATIONAL SPORTS EVENT SAW ITS FIRST WOMEN'S
    SOCCER TOURNAMENT IN 1996, WITH THE U.S. WINNING GOLD?

    a) The FIFA World Cup
    b) The Summer Olympics
    c) The Pan American Games
    d) The UEFA European Championship

23. WHICH LONG-RUNNING ANIMATED T.V. SHOW SET IN SPRINGFIELD FEATURED A YELLOW, DYSFUNCTIONAL FAMILY?

a) Family Guy
b) The Simpsons
c) King of the Hill
d) South Park

24. WHAT TRADING CARD GAME, INTRODUCED IN 1993, BECAME POPULAR AMONG FANTASY ENTHUSIASTS AND COMPETITIVE GAMERS?

a) Pokémon Trading Card Game
b) Magic: The Gathering
c) Dungeons & Dragons
d) Yu-Gi-Oh!

25. WHICH AMERICAN POP DIVA HAD HITS LIKE "VISION OF LOVE" AND "HERO" IN THE 1990S?

a) Whitney Houston
b) Mariah Carey
c) Celine Dion
d) Janet Jackson

26. WHAT POPULAR VIRTUAL PET TOY, RELEASED IN 1997, REQUIRED USERS TO FEED, PLAY WITH, AND CARE FOR THEIR PIXELATED PETS?

a) Polly Pocket
b) Tamagotchi
c) Beanie Babies
d) Furby

27. WHICH ALTERNATIVE ROCK BAND BECAME KNOWN FOR THEIR ANGST-FILLED ALBUM NEVERMIND AND "SMELLS LIKE TEEN SPIRIT"?

a) Pearl Jam
b) Nirvana
c) Radiohead
d) Soundgarden

28. WHAT EUROPEAN COUNTRY EXPERIENCED A BRUTAL CIVIL WAR
FOLLOWING ITS BREAKUP, LEADING TO THE DAYTON AGREEMENT
IN 1995?

a) Czechoslovakia
b) Bosnia and Herzegovina
c) Serbia
d) Yugoslavia

29. WHICH AMERICAN SITCOM STARRED WILL SMITH AS A TEENAGER
WHO MOVES FROM WEST PHILADELPHIA TO LIVE WITH HIS RICH
RELATIVES?

a) Family Matters
b) The Fresh Prince of Bel-Air
c) Full House
d) Different Strokes

30. WHAT MAJOR COMPUTER MANUFACTURER BECAME KNOWN FOR
ITS COLORFUL IMACS IN THE LATE 1990S?

a) IBM
b) Apple
c) HP
d) Dell

31. WHAT ANIMATED T.V. SHOW FEATURED THE ADVENTURES OF A
CAT AND A DOG CONJOINED AT THE WAIST?

a) Ren & Stimpy
b) CatDog
c) CatDog
d) Tom and Jerry

32. WHICH AMERICAN FEMALE ROCK SINGER PERFORMED HITS LIKE
"IRONIC" AND "YOU OUGHTA KNOW"?

a) Gwen Stefani
b) Alanis Morissette
c) Courtney Love
d) Sheryl Crow

33. WHAT GAMING CONSOLE BY NINTENDO BECAME FAMOUS FOR ITS ICONIC THREE-PRONGED CONTROLLER AND GAMES LIKE GOLDENEYE 007?

a) PlayStation
b) Nintendo 64
c) Sega Dreamcast
d) Sega Saturn

34. WHICH AMERICAN SINGER-SONGWRITER BROUGHT A LATIN INFLUENCE TO HER HITS "IF YOU HAD MY LOVE" AND "WAITING FOR TONIGHT"?

a) Shakira
b) Jennifer Lopez
c) Gloria Estefan
d) Selena

35. WHAT INTERNATIONAL ORGANIZATION WAS FOUNDED IN 1995 TO OVERSEE GLOBAL TRADE RULES AND RESOLVE DISPUTES?

a) United Nations
b) World Trade Organization
c) International Labour Organization
d) International Monetary Fund

36. WHICH AMERICAN BOY BAND BECAME A SENSATION WITH THEIR HITS "BYE BYE BYE" AND "TEARIN' UP MY HEART"?

a) Backstreet Boys
b) NSYNC
c) New Kids on the Block
d) Westlife

37. WHAT 1999 SCIENCE FICTION FILM INTRODUCED AUDIENCES TO A COMPUTER-GENERATED WORLD CALLED "THE MATRIX"?

a) Inception
b) The Matrix
c) Minority Report
d) Blade Runner

38. WHICH T.V. SHOW FEATURED THE ANTICS OF HOMER, MARGE, BART, LISA, AND MAGGIE IN THEIR FICTIONAL HOMETOWN?

a) Family Guy
b) The Simpsons
c) King of the Hill
d) South Park

39. WHAT GLOBAL EVENT SAW THE PEACEFUL REUNIFICATION OF EAST AND WEST GERMANY IN 1990?

a) The dissolution of the Soviet Union
b) The German reunification
c) The fall of the Berlin Wall
d) The end of the Cold War

40. WHICH AMERICAN PROFESSIONAL WRESTLER BECAME KNOWN FOR HIS "AUSTIN 3:16" CATCHPHRASE IN THE WWE?

a) The Rock
b) Stone Cold Steve Austin
c) John Cena
d) Hulk Hogan

41. WHICH TECH COMPANY LAUNCHED THE FIRST WIDELY AVAILABLE WEB BROWSER, NETSCAPE NAVIGATOR, IN THE 1990S?

a) Microsoft
b) Apple
c) Netscape
d) IBM

42. WHAT HIT SONG BY HANSON TOPPED THE CHARTS IN THE LATE 1990S WITH ITS CATCHY "MMMBOP" CHORUS?

a) Wannabe
b) MmmBop
c) I Want it That Way
d) No Scrubs

43. WHICH ANIMATED DISNEY FILM FOLLOWED A YOUNG LION CUB DESTINED TO BECOME KING OF THE SAVANNA?

a) Aladdin
b) Mulan
c) The Lion King
d) Pocahontas

44. WHICH TOY CRAZE HAD KIDS COLLECTING AND TRADING PLASTIC MONSTERS WITH DIFFERENT ELEMENTAL POWERS?

a) Pokémon
b) Beyblade
c) Digimon
d) Neopets

45. WHAT INTERNET SEARCH ENGINE, FOUNDED IN 1998 BY LARRY PAGE AND SERGEY BRIN, BECAME THE MOST POPULAR WAY TO FIND INFORMATION ONLINE?

a) Yahoo
b) Google
c) AltaVista
d) Lycos

46. WHICH AMERICAN CRIME DRAMA FOLLOWED THE LIVES OF BALTIMORE DETECTIVES AND THEIR BATTLE AGAINST DRUGS AND CORRUPTION?

a) The Wire
b) The Wire
c) Law & Order
d) NYPD Blue

47. WHICH EUROPEAN NATION SAW AN EXPLOSION IN ITS TECH INDUSTRY WITH THE DEVELOPMENT OF MOBILE PHONES AND TELECOMMUNICATION NETWORKS?

a) Germany
b) France
c) Finland
d) Sweden

48. WHICH POPULAR GAME SERIES, KNOWN FOR ITS SIDE-SCROLLING PLATFORMING LEVELS, INTRODUCED GAMERS TO MARIO AND LUIGI?

a) Sonic the Hedgehog
b) Super Mario Bros
c) Mega Man
d) Castlevania

49. WHAT ANIMATED T.V. SERIES BY MATT GROENING FOLLOWED A GROUP OF MISMATCHED CHARACTERS LIVING IN THE YEAR 3000?

a) The Simpsons
b) Futurama
c) American Dad
d) Family Guy

50. WHICH AMERICAN SINGER BECAME KNOWN FOR HER POP BALLADS "GENIE IN A BOTTLE" AND "WHAT A GIRL WANTS"?

a) Britney Spears
b) Christina Aguilera
c) Jessica Simpson
d) Mandy Moore

51. WHAT 1990S T.V. SITCOM FEATURED FRAN DRESCHER AS A NANNY CARING FOR THE CHILDREN OF A WEALTHY BROADWAY PRODUCER?

a) The Nanny
b) Friends
c) Full House
d) Mad About You

52. WHAT MAJOR TECH COMPANY POPULARIZED ONLINE SHOPPING WITH ITS "1-CLICK" BUYING FEATURE?

a) eBay
b) Amazon
c) Yahoo
d) Google

53. WHICH ANIMATED DISNEY FILM FEATURED THE ADVENTURES OF A NATIVE AMERICAN WOMAN AND HER LOVE FOR AN ENGLISH SETTLER?

a) Mulan
b) The Little Mermaid
c) Pocahontas
d) Aladdin

54. WHICH AMERICAN PUNK BAND ROSE TO FAME WITH THEIR ALBUM DOOKIE AND HITS LIKE "BASKET CASE"?

a) Nirvana
b) Green Day
c) Blink-182
d) The Offspring

55. WHICH POPULAR TOY CRAZE SAW KIDS RACING, TRADING, AND BATTLING THEIR BEYBLADES AGAINST EACH OTHER?

a) Pokémon
b) Digimon
c) Beyblade
d) Tamagotchi

56. WHAT EUROPEAN FOOTBALL LEAGUE BECAME KNOWN IN THE 1990S FOR ITS HIGH-PROFILE TRANSFERS, MERCHANDISING, AND INTERNATIONAL T.V. DEALS?

a) La Liga
b) Serie A
c) Bundesliga
d) Premier League

57. WHICH 1994 ROMANTIC COMEDY FEATURED HUGH GRANT AS A BUMBLING ENGLISHMAN NAVIGATING LOVE AT WEDDINGS?

a) Love Actually
b) Four Weddings and a Funeral
c) Notting Hill
d) Bridget Jones's Diary

58. WHAT WAS THE NAME OF THE YUGOSLAVIAN PRESIDENT WHO WAS TRIED FOR WAR CRIMES AT THE INTERNATIONAL CRIMINAL TRIBUNAL?

a) Nicolae Ceaușescu
b) Slobodan Milošević
c) Radovan Karadžić
d) Franjo Tuđman

59. WHICH JAPANESE ANIMATED SERIES INTRODUCED VIEWERS TO THE ADVENTURES OF GOKU AND HIS FRIENDS IN THE FIGHT AGAINST EVIL?

a) Naruto
b) Dragon Ball Z
c) One Piece
d) Bleach

60. WHAT MAJOR TV NETWORK LAUNCHED TRL, A DAILY COUNTDOWN SHOW FOR THE HOTTEST MUSIC VIDEOS OF THE 1990S?

a) ABC
b) CBS
c) MTV
d) NBC

61. WHICH AMERICAN POP BAND RELEASED THE ALBUM TRAGIC KINGDOM, FEATURING THE HIT SINGLE "DON'T SPEAK"?

a) The Cranberries
b) No Doubt
c) Spice Girls
d) TLC

62. WHAT ARCADE GAME BY SEGA HAD PLAYERS GUIDING A BLUE HEDGEHOG THROUGH LOOPS AND COLLECTING GOLDEN RINGS?

a) Mario Bros.
b) Sonic the Hedgehog
c) Street Fighter
d) Pac-Man

63. WHICH FORMER SOUTH AFRICAN PRESIDENT AND ANTI-APARTHEID LEADER WON THE NOBEL PEACE PRIZE AND BECAME A GLOBAL ICON IN THE 1990S?

a) Desmond Tutu
b) Nelson Mandela
c) Thabo Mbeki
d) Jacob Zuma

64. WHAT 1999 SCI-FI FILM STARRED BRUCE WILLIS AS A PSYCHOLOGIST HELPING A YOUNG BOY WHO COULD SEE DEAD PEOPLE?

a) The Sixth Sense
b) The Sixth Sense
c) Armageddon
d) Unbreakable

65. WHICH POPULAR '90S VIDEO GAME BY SQUARE FEATURED A YOUNG HERO NAMED CLOUD STRIFE AND BECAME A GLOBAL SENSATION?

a) Legend of Zelda
b) Super Mario 64
c) Final Fantasy VII
d) Metal Gear Solid

66. WHICH ANIMATED T.V. SHOW FEATURING TWO DIM-WITTED FAST-FOOD WORKERS BECAME A CULT HIT IN THE 1990S?

a) South Park
b) Beavis and Butt-Head
c) The Simpsons
d) King of the Hill

67. WHAT T.V. SERIES STARRED SARAH MICHELLE GELLAR AS A TEENAGE VAMPIRE SLAYER BATTLING EVIL FORCES?

a) Charmed
b) Buffy the Vampire Slayer
c) The X-Files
d) Supernatural

68. WHICH ALTERNATIVE ROCK BAND RELEASED THE ALBUM OK COMPUTER, EXPLORING THEMES OF CONSUMERISM AND ALIENATION?

a) Nirvana
b) Radiohead
c) Pearl Jam
d) Oasis

69. WHAT ONLINE VIDEO PLATFORM BECAME POPULAR FOR SHARING CLIPS, COMMERCIALS, AND USER-GENERATED CONTENT IN THE LATE 1990S?

a) Vimeo
b) YouTube
c) Dailymotion
d) Metacafe

70. WHICH COMPUTER GAME BY MAXIS ALLOWED PLAYERS TO CONTROL VIRTUAL PEOPLE AND BUILD THEIR DREAM HOMES AND NEIGHBORHOODS?

a) RollerCoaster Tycoon
b) The Sims
c) Civilization
d) Age of Empires

71. WHICH MIDDLE EASTERN TERRORIST ORGANIZATION GAINED NOTORIETY AFTER BOMBING U.S. EMBASSIES IN EAST AFRICA IN 1998?

a) Al-Qaeda
b) Hezbollah
c) Hamas
d) Islamic Jihad

72. WHICH EUROPEAN NATION EXPERIENCED A "VELVET DIVORCE," PEACEFULLY SPLITTING INTO TWO INDEPENDENT COUNTRIES IN 1993?

a) Yugoslavia
b) Czechoslovakia
c) Soviet Union
d) Germany

73. WHAT JAPANESE COMPANY RELEASED THE TAMAGOTCHI, A HANDHELD VIRTUAL PET, IN THE LATE 1990S?

a) Sony
b) Nintendo
c) Bandai
d) Sega

74. WHAT AMERICAN ANIMATED T.V. SERIES FOLLOWED THE ADVENTURES OF ARNOLD AND HIS FRIENDS IN A CITY NEIGHBORHOOD?

a) Doug
b) Hey Arnold!
c) Rugrats
d) Arthur

75. WHICH AMERICAN TEEN POP BAND PERFORMED HITS LIKE "MOTOWNPHILLY" AND "END OF THE ROAD"?

a) NSYNC
b) Backstreet Boys
c) Boyz II Men
d) New Kids on the Block

76. WHAT 1995 PIXAR FILM BECAME THE FIRST FULL-LENGTH ANIMATED MOVIE TO BE COMPLETELY COMPUTER-GENERATED?

a) A Bug's Life
b) Toy Story
c) Monsters, Inc.
d) Finding Nemo

77. WHICH CANADIAN ROCK BAND RELEASED THE ALBUM JAGGED LITTLE PILL, EARNING ACCLAIM FOR ITS RAW LYRICS AND ENERGETIC SOUND?

a) Shania Twain
b) Celine Dion
c) Alanis Morissette
d) Bryan Adams

78. WHAT LONG-RUNNING REALITY T.V. SERIES FOLLOWED CONTESTANTS STRANDED ON A TROPICAL ISLAND COMPETING FOR A CASH PRIZE?

a) Big Brother
b) The Amazing Race
c) Survivor
d) Fear Factor

79. WHICH JAPANESE ARTIST BECAME A GLOBAL PHENOMENON FOR HER PAINTINGS, INSTALLATIONS, AND "INFINITY MIRRORED ROOMS"?

a) Takashi Murakami
b) Yayoi Kusama
c) Ai Weiwei
d) Haruki Murakami

80. WHAT BRITISH POP BAND PERFORMED THE HITS "WANNABE" AND "SAY YOU'LL BE THERE," BECOMING AN INTERNATIONAL SENSATION?

a) Atomic Kitten
b) Spice Girls
c) All Saints
d) Sugababes

81. WHICH AMERICAN RAPPER AND BUSINESSMAN BECAME KNOWN FOR HIS ALBUM REASONABLE DOUBT AND HIS CLOTHING BRAND ROCAWEAR?

a) Dr. Dre
b) Snoop Dogg
c) Jay-Z
d) Nas

82. WHAT 1993 FILM STARRING TOM HANKS AND MEG RYAN TOLD THE STORY OF TWO PEOPLE FINDING LOVE THROUGH A RADIO PROGRAM?

a) When Harry Met Sally
b) Sleepless in Seattle
c) You've Got Mail
d) The American President

83. WHICH AMERICAN T.V. SERIES FEATURED A GROUP OF TEENAGE WITCHES LEARNING ABOUT THEIR POWERS WHILE DEALING WITH HIGH SCHOOL DRAMA?

a) Charmed
b) Sabrina, the Teenage Witch
c) Buffy the Vampire Slayer
d) The Craft

84. WHICH BRITISH VIDEO GAME DEVELOPER CREATED TOMB RAIDER, INTRODUCING PLAYERS TO THE ADVENTURES OF LARA CROFT?

a) Rare
b) Core Design
c) Bullfrog Productions
d) Psygnosis

85. WHICH U.S NETWORK LAUNCHED SOUTH PARK, FEATURING THE ANTICS OF FOUR BOYS IN THE FICTIONAL TOWN OF SOUTH PARK, COLORADO?

a) NBC
b) ABC
c) Comedy Central
d) Fox

86. WHAT FASHION TREND SAW KIDS WEARING FLANNEL SHIRTS, RIPPED JEANS, AND DOC MARTENS IN THE 1990S?

a) Hip Hop
b) Grunge
c) Preppy
d) Sporty

87. WHICH 1998 PIXAR FILM FOLLOWED A GROUP OF INSECTS SEEKING HELP FROM CIRCUS PERFORMERS TO DEFEND THEIR COLONY?

a) Toy Story
b) A Bug's Life
c) Monsters, Inc.
d) Finding Nemo

88. WHAT ONLINE MUSIC SERVICE ALLOWED USERS TO DOWNLOAD AND SHARE SONGS ILLEGALLY IN THE LATE 1990S?

a) iTunes
b) Napster
c) Spotify
d) Pandora

89. WHICH AMERICAN BOY BAND RELEASED THE ALBUM MILLENNIUM, BREAKING RECORDS WITH HITS LIKE "I WANT IT THAT WAY"?

a) Boyz II Men
b) Backstreet Boys
c) NSYNC
d) 98 Degrees

90. WHAT 1994 COMEDY FEATURED JIM CARREY AS A DIM-WITTED DETECTIVE TASKED WITH FINDING THE MIAMI DOLPHINS' MISSING MASCOT?

a) The Mask
b) Ace Ventura: Pet Detective
c) Dumb and Dumber
d) Liar Liar

91. WHICH EUROPEAN COUNTRY EMERGED AS A HIGH-TECH HUB DUE TO GOVERNMENT POLICIES AND FOREIGN INVESTMENT IN THE 1990S?

a) Ireland
b) Finland
c) Portugal
d) Belgium

92. WHICH JAPANESE ANIME FILM DIRECTED BY HAYAO MIYAZAKI INTRODUCED AUDIENCES TO THE SPIRIT WORLD AND A YOUNG GIRL NAMED CHIHIRO?

a) Princess Mononoke
b) Spirited Away
c) My Neighbor Totoro
d) Kiki's Delivery Service

93. WHAT AMERICAN BASEBALL PLAYER BROKE ROGER MARIS' HOME RUN RECORD BY HITTING 70 HOME RUNS IN THE 1998 SEASON?

a) Derek Jeter
b) Mark McGwire
c) Sammy Sosa
d) Barry Bonds

94. WHICH 1999 ANIMATED T.V. SHOW BY SETH MACFARLANE FOLLOWED THE LIVES OF PETER GRIFFIN AND HIS DYSFUNCTIONAL FAMILY?

a) The Simpsons
b) Family Guy
c) King of the Hill
d) American Dad

95. WHICH 1995 SCIENCE FICTION FILM FEATURED BRUCE WILLIS AND BRAD PITT NAVIGATING A POST-APOCALYPTIC FUTURE WITH TIME TRAVEL?

a) Total Recall
b) 12 Monkeys
c) Blade Runner
d) The Fifth Element

96. WHAT SPORTS LEAGUE INTRODUCED A "DREAM TEAM" OF NBA PLAYERS IN THE 1992 OLYMPICS?

a) NFL
b) NHL
c) MLB
d) NBA

97. WHICH BRITISH ALTERNATIVE BAND RELEASED PARKLIFE, LEADING TO THE "BRITPOP" MOVEMENT OF THE 1990S?

a) Oasis
b) Blur
c) The Verve
d) Pulp

98. WHAT HANDHELD GAMING DEVICE BY NINTENDO ALLOWED PLAYERS TO BATTLE AND TRADE CREATURES KNOWN AS POKÉMON?

a) PlayStation Portable
b) Game Boy
c) Sega Game Gear
d) Atari Lynx

99. WHICH AMERICAN ROCK BAND RELEASED THE ALBUM CRASH, BLENDING ALTERNATIVE ROCK WITH JAZZ AND JAM BAND INFLUENCES?

a) Phish
b) Dave Matthews Band
c) Counting Crows
d) Hootie & the Blowfish

100. WHICH CANADIAN ALTERNATIVE ROCK BAND RELEASED TRAGIC KINGDOM AND BECAME KNOWN FOR THEIR HIGH-ENERGY SKA-PUNK HITS?

a) Rush
b) Nickelback
c) No Doubt
d) Barenaked Ladies

101. WHAT AMERICAN SOFTWARE COMPANY RELEASED THE FIRST VERSION OF INTERNET EXPLORER, SPARKING THE BROWSER WARS OF THE 1990S?

a) Apple
b) Microsoft
c) Netscape
d) IBM

102. WHICH AMERICAN ACTOR STARRED IN MOVIES LIKE FORREST
GUMP, SAVING PRIVATE RYAN, AND APOLLO 13 IN THE 1990S?

   a) Brad Pitt
   b) Tom Hanks
   c) Leonardo DiCaprio
   d) Johnny Depp

103. WHICH RAP GROUP RELEASED THE ALBUM THE SCORE,
BLENDING HIP-HOP WITH REGGAE AND JAZZ INFLUENCES?

   a) Wu-Tang Clan
   b) A Tribe Called Quest
   c) The Fugees
   d) OutKast

104. WHAT AMERICAN SITCOM STARRED KELSEY GRAMMER AS A
RADIO PSYCHIATRIST LIVING IN SEATTLE?

   a) Friends
   d) Seinfeld
   c) Frasier
   d) Cheers

105. WHICH AMERICAN R&B GROUP PERFORMED HITS LIKE
"WATERFALLS" AND "NO SCRUBS"?

   a) Destiny's Child
   b) TLC
   c) En Vogue
   d) Salt-N-Pepa

106. WHICH VIDEO GAME FRANCHISE HAD PLAYERS CONTROLLING A
GROUP OF HEROIC SOLDIERS FIGHTING AN ALIEN INVASION?

   a) Halo
   b) X-COM
   c) StarCraft
   d) Doom

107. WHAT EUROPEAN FOOTBALL CLUB BECAME KNOWN FOR THEIR DOMINANCE IN THE CHAMPIONS LEAGUE AND THEIR "GALACTICOS"?

    a) Manchester United
    b) AC Milan
    c) Real Madrid
    d) Bayern Munich

108. WHICH AMERICAN ANIMATED FILM ABOUT TALKING TOYS INTRODUCED AUDIENCES TO WOODY, BUZZ LIGHTYEAR, AND THEIR FRIENDS?

    a)A Bug's Life
    b) Toy Story
    c) The Incredibles
    d) Monsters, Inc.

109. WHAT VIDEO GAME SERIES BY CAPCOM HAD PLAYERS FIGHTING OFF ZOMBIES IN A MANSION AND UNCOVERING A PHARMACEUTICAL CONSPIRACY?

    a) Metal Gear Solid
    b) Silent Hill
    c) Resident Evil
    d) Tomb Raider

110. WHICH REALITY T.V. SHOW FEATURED FAMILIES RENOVATING THEIR HOMES WITH THE HELP OF AN ECCENTRIC TEAM OF DESIGNERS?

    a) Fixer Upper
    b) House Hunters
    c) Trading Spaces
    d) Extreme Makeover: Home Edition

111. WHICH AMERICAN COMEDIAN BECAME KNOWN FOR HIS OVER-THE-TOP SKETCHES AND IMPRESSIONS ON IN LIVING COLOR?

a) Chris Rock
b) Eddie Murphy
c) Jim Carrey
d) Dave Chappelle

112. WHAT 1998 ANIMATED FILM FOLLOWED THE JOURNEY OF A GIRL WHO DISCOVERS SHE IS THE LOST PRINCESS OF RUSSIA?

a) Mulan
b) Anastasia
c) The Prince of Egypt
d) Hercules

113. WHICH AMERICAN SCI-FI SERIES STARRED DAVID DUCHOVNY AND GILLIAN ANDERSON AS FBI AGENTS INVESTIGATING THE SUPERNATURAL?

a) Buffy the Vampire Slayer
b) The X-Files
c) Charmed
d) Supernatural

114. WHICH EUROPEAN NATION BECAME KNOWN FOR ITS HIGH-SPEED INTERNET AND TECH STARTUPS AFTER ADOPTING PRO-INNOVATION POLICIES?

a) Germany
b) France
c) Estonia
d) Sweden

115. WHAT WAS THE NAME OF THE FIRST SUCCESSFUL MAMMAL CLONE, BORN IN SCOTLAND IN 1996?

a) Dolly
b) Daisy
c) Molly
d) Polly

116. WHICH AMERICAN ANIMATED SERIES CREATED BY BUTCH HARTMAN FOLLOWED A BOY WHO GAINS FAIRY GODPARENTS?

   a) The Simpsons
   b) The Fairly Odd Parents
   c) Adventure Time
   d) SpongeBob SquarePants

117. WHICH JAPANESE VIDEO GAME COMPANY RELEASED FINAL FANTASY VII, ONE OF THE BEST-SELLING RPGS EVER?

   a) Nintendo
   b) Square Enix
   c) Capcom
   d) Konami

118. WHICH GLOBAL POP STAR BECAME KNOWN FOR HER ICONIC OUTFIT AND ANTHEM ...BABY ONE MORE TIME?

   a) Madonna
   b) Britney Spears
   c) Christina Aguilera
   d) Jessica Simpson

119. WHAT WAS THE NAME OF THE FIRST SEARCH ENGINE TO USE AN ALGORITHM THAT RANKED RESULTS BASED ON LINKS AND RELEVANCE?

   a) Yahoo
   b) Google
   c) AltaVista
   d) Lycos

120. WHICH JAPANESE HORROR FILM BY HIDEO NAKATA INTRODUCED AUDIENCES TO A CURSED VIDEOTAPE THAT LED TO TERRIFYING CONSEQUENCES?

   a) The Grudge
   b) Ring
   c) Dark Water
   d) Pulse

1990s Trivia Answers

1. d) Oasis

2. a) Jurassic Park

3. b) Friends

4. c) Tupac Shakur

5. b) Quake

6. b) Aladdin

7. c) Sony PlayStation

8. a) Oprah Winfrey

9. b) The X-Files

10. b) The Powerpuff Girls

11. a) Titanic

12. b) The Summer Olympics

13. b) Backstreet Boys

14. b) J.K. Rowling

15. b) eBay

16. b) Saved by the Bell

17. b) Beavis and Butt-Head

18. b) Bill Clinton

19. b) Britney Spears

20. b) Microsoft

21. b) Seinfeld

22. b) The Summer Olympics

23. b) The Simpsons

24. b) Magic: The Gathering

25. b) Mariah Carey

26. b) Tamagotchi

27. b) Nirvana

28. b) Bosnia and Herzegovina

29. b) The Fresh Prince of Bel-Air

30. b) Apple

31. b) CatDog

32. b) Alanis Morissette

33. b) Nintendo 64

34. b) Jennifer Lopez

35. b) World Trade Organization

36. b) NSYNC

37. b) The Matrix

38. b) The Simpsons

39. b) The German reunification

40. b) Stone Cold Steve Austin

41. c) Netscape

42. b) MmmBop

43. c) The Lion King

44. a) Pokémon

45. b) Google

46. b) The Wire

47. c) Finland

48. b) Super Mario Bros.

49. b) Futurama

50. b) Christina Aguilera

51. a) The Nanny

52. b) Amazon

53. c) Pocahontas

54. b) Green Day

55. c) Beyblade

56. d) Premier League

57. b) Four Weddings and a Funeral

58. b) Slobodan Milošević

59. b) Dragon Ball Z

60. c) MTV

61. b) No Doubt

62. b) Sonic the Hedgehog

63. b) Nelson Mandela

64. a) The Sixth Sense

65. c) Final Fantasy VII

66. b) Beavis and Butt-Head

67. b) Buffy the Vampire Slayer

68. b) Radiohead

69. d) Metacafe

70. b) The Sims

71. a) Al-Qaeda

72. b) Czechoslovakia

73. c) Bandai

74. b) Hey Arnold!

75. c) Boyz II Men

76. b) Toy Story

77. c) Alanis Morissette

78. c) Survivor

79. b) Yayoi Kusama

80. b) Spice Girls

81. c) Jay-Z

82. b) Sleepless in Seattle

83. b) Sabrina, the Teenage Witch

84. b) Core Design

85. c) Comedy Central

86. b) Grunge

87. b) A Bug's Life

88. b) Napster

89. b) Backstreet Boys

90. b) Ace Ventura: Pet Detective

91. a) Ireland

92. b) Spirited Away

93. b) Mark McGwire

94. b) Family Guy

95. b) 12 Monkeys

96. d) NBA

97. b) Blur

98. b) Game Boy

99. b) Dave Matthews Band

100. c) No Doubt

101. b) Microsoft

102. b) Tom Hanks

103. c) The Fugees

104. c) Frasier

105. b) TLC

106. b) X-COM

107. c) Real Madrid

108. b) Toy Story

109. c) Resident Evil

110. c) Trading Spaces

111. c) Jim Carrey

112. b) Anastasia

113. b) The X-Files

114. c) Estonia

115. a) Dolly

116. b) The Fairly OddParents

117. b) Square Enix

118. b) Britney Spears

119. c) AltaVista

120. b) Ringu

CONCLUSION

And Reflection

CONCLUSION AND REFLECTION

The 1950s saw rock and roll take over the hearts of young people, and war and public issues were about to transform political life. Space flight and counterculture phenomena of the late '60s'60s mobilized society's awareness in pursuit of equality as civil rights protests emerged.

The decade of the 1970s1970s said, "Hello, discriminating tastes! 21st-century, discriminating tastes! 21st-century fashionable grooving and film productions like Star Wars changed movies forever. The Watergate affair did not stop the resistance movements. By the 1980s1980s, featuring MTV and the brightness of neon lights, there were music icons such as Michael Jackson and Madonna. Games machines and VHS overshadowed entertainment while technology was embraced.

In the 1990s, the Digital Age made way for the Internet and PlayStation console games. Grunge and hip-hop turned the music on its head, while cinema, led by Harry Potter movies and The Matrix, shaped current popular culture. The reunion of Germany showed the period of a new political.

Like a time trip, we laughed, forgot, and remembered as we jogged down memory lane of the entire presence within the confines of the campus. Every time mu, sic, film, and technology craft our present and will be our guide, passing down stories, congratulating victories, and studying histories.

SOURCES OR REFERENCE

Books

Friedan, B. (1963). The Feminine Mystique. W. W. Norton & Company.

Haley, A. (1976). Roots: The Saga of an American Family. Doubleday.

Kerouac, J. (1957). On the Road. Viking Press.

King, S. (1977). The Shining. Doubleday.

McLuhan, M. (1964). Understanding Media: The Extensions of Man. McGraw-Hill.

Salinger, J. D. (1951). The Catcher in the Rye. Little, Brown and Company.

Stoker, S. (1999). The Matrix and Philosophy: Welcome to the Desert of the Real. Open Court.

Wells, J. (1992). The Official Guide to The X-Files. HarperPrism.

Journal Articles

Cohen, L. (1996). From Town Center to Shopping Center: The Reconfiguration of Community Marketplaces in Postwar America. American Historical Review, 101(4), 1050-1081.

Diner, H. (1983). American Jewry and the Great War. American Jewish History, 72(2), 140-154.

Jones, S. (1997). MTV and the Globalization of Popular Culture. International Journal of Cultural Studies, 1(1), 59-72.

Meyrowitz, J. (1986). Television and Interpersonal Behavior: Codes of Perception and Response. Communication Research, 13(1), 35-57.

Thompson, E. P. (1978). The Poverty of Theory or an Orrery of Errors. New Left Review, 1(118), 5-31.

Websites

American Civil Liberties Union. (2018). Civil Rights in the 1960s. https://www.aclu.org/1960s-civil-rights.

National Aeronautics and Space Administration (NASA). (2019). Apollo Program. https://www.nasa.gov/apollo.

The New York Times. (2020). The Berlin Wall Falls in 1989. https://archive.nytimes.com/berlin-wall-falls-1989.

Made in the USA
Middletown, DE
16 December 2024